THE WRITING ROAD TO READING

The
WRITING
ROAD
To
READING

A Modern Method of Phonics for Teaching Children to Read

By

Romalda Bishop Spalding

with

Walter T. Spalding

Whiteside, Inc., and William Morrow & Company

New York, 1957

CONTENTS

INTRODUCTION

THE PURPOSE of this book is to present in complete and workable detail the Unified Phonics Method for teaching children correct and accurate speech, writing, spelling, and reading. This is the method which I have developed and used exclusively during the past twenty years. Throughout this long period of vigorous testing—in all the elementary grades and in the tutoring of hundreds of individuals with language disabilities—I have found it equally applicable to *home* and *school* use, and as practicable for a single pupil as for an entire class. And though the method was designed especially for use in the elementary schools beginning with the first grade, it has proved to be fully successful in high school classrooms and in private instruction from pre-school age through college age, and even older. Indeed, anyone with a deficiency in reading and spelling can benefit from the Unified Phonics Method regardless of age.

At the outset I think it important to state several things which the method is *not:*

It does *not* advocate the old-fashioned phonics commonly taught thirty years ago and now being partially revived in many American schools.

The Unified Phonics Method, with its new approach and its improved, simplified phonics, is *not* merely a useful adjunct to the sight method of teaching.

The Unified Phonics Method has proved its usefulness for children with language deficiencies, but it is *not* primarily a technique for remedial reading—that costly, widespread and frightening proof of the faulty teaching of beginning readers today.

It is not merely another alternate and theoretical approach to the reading problem.

The Unified Phonics Method *is* a fully developed, highly success-ful and complete method for teaching the basic techniques of the lan-guage arts—accurate speaking, spelling, writing and reading—as one integrated subject.

Practical experience has convinced me that any child physically and mentally qualified to enter school at the age of six is fully able, willing and eager to learn to write and read if he is taught by this logical approach to language. The professional concept of "reading readiness" is accordingly immaterial. Ideally, therefore, this teaching method should be instituted in the first grade, and the beginning reader should not be confused by simultaneous exposure to any other method of teaching.

The core of the method is a technique by which the child learns how to write down the sounds used in spoken English as they are com-bined into words. Thus, conversely he can pronounce any printed word. Meaning is thoroughly taught hand-in-hand with the writing and by using new words in original sentences. It begins with correct pronun-ciation of words and the writing of their component sounds in accord-ance with the rules of English spelling. By this means the saying, writ-ing, reading and meaning of words are well learned and understood. After this initial grounding, a child in his reading recognizes words at a glance—very soon without any resort to their phonetic composi-tion. For reading there is no resort to pictures or any other aids ex-cept the use of phonics. After a new word has been read aloud its mean-ing is discussed and pictures are used if they can help explain the meaning.

Thus far, I have stressed the ideal situation in which the Uni-fied Phonics Method is used exclusively to teach reading to beginners, and as such I recommend it to all elementary school teachers and school systems having freedom to act. As the world knows, elementary school teachers by and large are overworked and underpaid; but also they are dedicated men and women who devote their lives to the all-im-portant task of equipping youngsters with the basic tools of learning.

Their finest reward is their pleasure in seeing the eager minds of children develop keenness and strength. If teachers are bewildered by the theories and countertheories that mark the present controversy over the teaching of reading in our schools, if they feel that methods presently in vogue are less than satisfactory for the majority of their pupils, they should find in the Unified Phonics Method the answer to their problems. In similar situations I recommend it to parents who wish to start their children on the road to reading *before* formal schooling begins. For some children, the age of four is not too young.

We live, however, in a real world, and the ideal situation, I realize, will not materialize overnight. Accordingly, therefore, though I have said that the Unified Phonics Method is not primarily intended for remedial or supplementary use, I can also attest to its success when so used. Parents who are troubled by the realization that their children have fallen below the already too low "normal" accomplishments of American school children in reading and writing have here a method which they can practice successfully at home to overcome the deficiency. It is equally valuable to remedial or group teachers at any point.

The book, then, is recommended—and, yes, dedicated—to both teachers and parents. The ultimate dedication, of course, is to the school children of America themselves, whose right it is that they be given the means to master those basic tools of learning, the three R's. Without the three R's the developing and productive use of the mind, the habit of mental self-discipline and self-education, and, indeed, any real appreciation of our cultural heritage are impossible.

There is widespread controversy today as to the first objective of the schools' educational program. There are many educators, for example, who argue that the primary, if not sole, aim is the adjustment of the child to his environment. Others argue as strongly that the first consideration in school is learning and intellectual development. I stand with the latter to the extent that I believe that teaching the three R's and other intellectual techniques and disciplines is the first responsibility of our schools. No other agency is charged with this vital job.

The social adjustment of each to his fellow is the important duty of parents, but it should be the secondary aim of the teacher because adjustment is a matter equally shared with the home, the church, and other agencies. The formal education of children should be centered on the development of their highest individual ability to reason and think for themselves and on the inculcation of the desire to learn. Their education should also express a deep regard for high standards of work and for high ideals and moral values. The very life of our free world depends upon our children's intellectual development and intellectual integrity.

The attainment of these goals, given the right methods, is perhaps easier than we think. Children need and naturally desire reasoned discipline, strong guidance, and leadership from their elders. They need and want to be held to high standards of performance. And without these things "social adjustment" may well be somewhat meaningless.

I have reached these general conclusions along with my specific teaching method during some twenty-five years of study and work which included the usual courses required of the teaching profession and many advanced courses in the teaching of reading at Columbia and Harvard Universities. I have had continuous practical teaching experience in the Katherine Branson School, California, the Birch-Wathen School, New York, the Bronxville, N.Y. Public Schools, and Shady Hill School, Cambridge. I have taught every elementary grade. On the way, I have become indebted to many people.

I am basically, and most gratefully, indebted to the late Dr. Samuel T. Orton, eminent neurologist and brain specialist of New York, for his years of research and discoveries and of teaching in this field. It was my privilege, after having taken profitless courses from a number of reading "experts," to teach a Bronxville school boy directly under Dr. Orton for almost three years. His theory of the functioning of the brain in speaking, writing and reading and his application of this theory to overcome confusions were not only clear and logical but highly effective in practice. His book, READING, WRITING AND SPEECH PROB-

LEMS IN CHILDREN (W. W. Norton & Company, Inc., New York, 1937) covers this from the medical viewpoint. My contribution has been to simplify and expedite the application of his ideas to classroom teaching techniques through the many years of trial and patient practice. The value of Dr. Orton's pioneering work in the field cannot be overestimated.

Many classroom teachers and school principals have taken the course I have given on the Unified Phonics Method. They have conducted long and accurate experiments with it. In twenty-four schools in Hawaii it is now being used exclusively in the first, second and third grades. To all of these teachers and to their school superintendents, I am deeply indebted. Their devoted study, accurate teaching, and enthusiasm over the results have been a constant satisfaction.

I am grateful also to Mrs. Samuel T. Orton for her permission to use in this book facsimiles of the phonogram cards which I was given by Dr. Orton.

Further, I wish to acknowledge my gratitude to the Educational Testing Service of Princeton, New Jersey, and the Russell Sage Foundation for kindly consenting to my use of the Ayres list of words from the AYRES MEASURING SCALE FOR ABILITY IN SPELLING.

Acknowledgment is also due the grateful parents of the hundreds of children with reading troubles whom I have taught individually. These parents have in large measure inspired me to put my teaching into book form. Perhaps I owe a debt most of all to these hundreds of children and to those in my many classrooms. Every one of them has worked with me, used his mind—and shown me just how it is that children learn best how to comprehend and use the written and spoken language.

CHAPTER I

Teaching the Language Arts Today—The Basic Problem

THE CHILD, or the adult, who cannot easily read *and write* better English with a larger vocabulary than he normally uses in speaking, badly needs better teaching. Of course, this cannot apply to six-year-olds in their first year of school, but the groundwork for their facility with language should be laid in that first year. Many American first-grade teachers today would not concur with my conviction that every six-year-old who is sufficiently normal to be admitted to a school classroom is both willing and able to learn to read, write and spell. It is only true, in fact, when a simple, direct, logical and accurate method of teaching the language arts is used. The aim of this book is to provide just that. This book offers in the Unified Phonics Method an entirely different, but thoroughly tested approach to a phonics method of teaching writing, spelling and reading derived from accurate speaking.

Nothing in education is more vital to the future of America than that *all* its children shall learn to read and write easily, rapidly, accurately and enjoyably. A man who is not fairly well read in these changing times cannot pull his weight and be a competent member of our democracy. Everyone will agree that reading and writing ability is fundamental to every branch of education, and especially to self-education, all through life.

The Unified Phonics Method is one of learning by reasoning, rather than by memorizing alone. It comes at a time when a great many parents, and the American public generally, are justly alarmed at the failure of the schools to teach adequately the reading, writing, spelling and speaking of English to a high percentage of their children.

For example, the New York *World-Telegram* reported in its issue of December 13, 1955, that tests administered in fifty or more academic high schools in New York City had disclosed that over half of the students entering high school the preceding September were reading below their normal grade level. Specifically, 52.6% of the 18,711 pupils who entered from elementary schools were shown to be reading under par, and for the 25,587 who entered from junior high schools the percentage was 56.5%—an average for the entire group of 54.8% below the norm. The students' deficiencies ranged from just below normal to a shocking six years under par. Nor were the deficiencies confined to students of mediocre ability. Bernard E. Donovan, administrative director of the high-school division, who analyzed the test scores, was quoted as stating: "Retardation in reading, in terms of potential ability, is not confined to the lower ability groups. Its presence among pupils of superior mental ability is as prevalent."

It seems obvious to add that these data do not reflect a purely local problem. Mrs. Elisabeth A. Simpson, Director of the Reading Service, Institute of Psychological Services, Illinois Institute of Technology, reports in her 1954 publication, HELPING HIGH-SCHOOL STUDENTS READ BETTER, that the *Trexler Silent Reading Test,* when given to 7,380 *eighth*-grade graduates in the St. Louis public schools, revealed that three out of ten were reading at the *sixth*-grade level or below. It is widely known, furthermore, that the military authorities continue to be greatly disturbed by the fact that a high percentage of men otherwise fully competent for military service are handicapped because of their inability to read or write simple English. Special training classes have had to be organized to teach very elementary reading, writing, and arithmetic to draftees. Among these, of course, are persons who speak or read only a foreign language; but after proper allowance has been made for them, there still remain a large number with American background who simply were not taught to read in school. Indeed, who cannot call to mind intelligent boys or girls who have been unable to get a complete education because of a lack of facility with the basic tools of learning? Who cannot think of someone whose normal ambitions have been impeded simply because he or she did not learn to read or write competently in elementary school?

In his 1955 report on delinquency to the Mayor of New York City, the former Deputy Mayor, the Honorable Henry Epstein, struck an even grimmer note when he declared on page 18 of the report:

> Reading retardation is one of the special handicaps often associated with juvenile delinquency. The retarded reader is unable to meet other children on equal terms since he is materially handicapped in the area of activity that consumes the largest single block of his waking hours. As he moves into the high grades ability to read becomes essential to any other kind of learning—text books and other printed material become the major tool.
>
> The child who can't make a "go" of things in school gets more and more into a rut of failure and frustration. He becomes insecure, hostile, rebellious . . .
>
> The Board of Educational Personnel who know this field agree that: "failure in reading accounts more than any other single factor for behavior problems, truancy, and general school failure." . . . As of four years ago . . . 80% of those entering vocational high schools were a year or more retarded in reading.

Certainly it is not fair to look on non-readers or retarded readers as potential juvenile delinquents; yet we must recognize failure in school as a contributory cause of delinquency. The seeds of frustration and insecurity are sown too often in the elementary grades by failure to master reading and writing, and the unhappy, brooding child seeks an escape. To compensate for his failure, a child often becomes a bully or a truant, acquires hostility, or moves toward open rebellion, all of which can point in the dangerous direction of delinquency. The larger number who fail become shy and withdraw from every situation which might expose their weakness. As the happy, secure child is seldom a problem, we must strive in every way to make each child as free from failure as possible.

Any human situation is necessarily complex, and the factors affecting it are not always easy to isolate. Nonetheless, it must be said that the presence in our schools of an unhealthy percentage of retarded readers is due in large measure to reliance upon the so-called "sight method" as the principal technique sanctioned by professional educators for the teaching of reading. Its ascendancy came about in a rather strange way.

After the turn of the century many elementary school educators were influenced by the pragmatic philosophies of Dr. John Dewey of Columbia University. Dr. Dewey revolted against abstract learning; he thought of education as a tool which should enable an individual to integrate his culture and his vocation effectively. Justly, his contribution to the progressive school movement has won world-wide recognition, and his influence has been a strong factor in turning from the former reliance upon authoritarian methods toward the increasing emphasis upon learning through practice and experimentation. But in their zeal to apply Dr. Dewey's theories and to change old ways of teaching for interesting new ways in the 1920's, educators, in general, went overboard in making radical changes in the method of teaching reading and spelling.

It is true that the old pre-progressive way of teaching these subjects by phonics was neither scientific nor complete, and it was encumbered by tedious, ineffective drills. However, instead of these obvious faults being corrected, the whole phonics system was discarded and the sight method adopted. Before long most schools were attempting to teach children literally to memorize the *appearance* of every word, without the slightest regard for the sounds which the letters in sequence were meant to convey. In short, that great invention of the early Phoenicians, the letters of the alphabet as the symbols for sounds, was practically forsaken. In effect we reverted part way to the picture language of three thousand years ago. Every single word was to be seen as a whole and its "looks" were to be memorized. The child could not sound out the letters in sequence and thus recognize a word he had often heard spoken. He had not the least idea of what sounds the letters represented. Only last week I was teaching an eighth-grade girl who was almost completely ignorant of the fact that letters in English words represent certain distinct sounds. In this ignorance she was typical of the majority of our children in school, both public and private.

As I have intimated, this prevalent method of teaching reading in the American schools is called the "whole word recognition" or "sight" method as distinguished from the "sound" or phonics method. There are only these two, though educators often speak of there being many. The meaning of a word must be taught in either method, independently of the means by which the word is identified or recognized in print. Indeed, no other approach to reading the printed word is possible.

There are some children who learn to read very well, even to spell fairly well, under the sight method of teaching. These children, often numbering between one quarter and one third of a class, are those who are blessed with an excellent visual memory. In time they discover for themselves some of the connections between the letters and the sounds. Thus they derive a sort of homemade phonics, and the success of this fraction of the total number of pupils partly explains the confidence of many able teachers in the sight method.

But success for a minority is neither efficient nor enough.

Jacques Maritain, in his Terry lectures at Yale on the subject, "Education at the Crossroads," stated that what is learned should never be mechanically received as dead information but must be transformed by understanding into the very life of the mind. Reason which receives knowledge in a servile manner does not really know and is only depressed by a knowledge which is not its own, but that of others. On the contrary, reason which assimilates knowledge vitally

—that is, in a free, liberating manner—really knows and is exalted by this knowledge, which henceforth is its own. Then it is that reason really masters the things learned.

Let us look at the application of this statement upon the average six-year-old who enters a school where the sight method is in vogue. His first contact with the written word is the teacher's statement that the three letters c-a-t printed close together mean cat, or that the five letters h-o-u-s-e mean house. He is not given any reason why these combinations should mean what he is told they do mean, any more than he is given a reason for the thousands of other combinations of letters into words which he must memorize. He has the teacher's word for it, but he can see no logic, no reason why any of the combinations should have the meanings claimed for them. The letters to him have no relation whatever to the sound of the word. Thus this knowledge is never his own by means of his reason. It remains dead knowledge easily forgotten, uninteresting and appalling in the endless volume of it.

In time the beginner is introduced to the first in the series of ingeniously calibrated readers which constitute the chief tool of the teacher dedicated to the sight method. Once the lure of their brightly colored pictures is exhausted these sight-method readers are necessarily dull and infantile in content. For their fundamental purpose is, again, simply to fix in the child's mind the overall appearance of a few selected words at a time. In each day's lesson only a very few new words are introduced, and in the "story" for the day these words are repeated over and over again. Such "stories" must be built up artificially, of course, and the result is that their content is reduced to the average three-year-old's level of interest and understanding, and the six- or seven-year-old who must cope with it finds it unworthy of his serious attention or effort. The child being taught to read by the sight method, particularly if he is not encouraged and aided at home, can only conclude that reading is a dull occupation indeed. Because early impressions are vivid ones, this conclusion may well be a lasting one for the very many who simply cannot learn by the sight method.

After two or three years of this memorization, his teacher may let him have a limited and vague idea of the phonetic basis on which the written words he has been exposed to were all formed. By that late time, however, it is necessary to overcome the deep-seated frustration and hatred of reading which very many children have already acquired. Even for many of those who can memorize thousands of words, this is their first inkling that there is logic and a plan to the written language.

On the other hand, when a six-year-old child is introduced to the written language, he already has acquired at least a speaking vocabulary of between one and three thousand words. He, therefore, finds it novel and exciting to learn through phonics teaching to make certain characters on paper express the same sounds he uses in the words he knows. In manuscript writing these letters are almost identical with those he sees on the printed page. The whole vast world of letters thus makes sense to him. It is logical and understandable to him if from the first he is taught to write down the letters which express the sounds he speaks —that is, if he spells the words by writing their *sounds*. Reading those words follows almost automatically. He uses reasoning rather than pure rote memorizing in both his spelling and reading. His learning becomes an exciting, challenging experience.

In contrast to undisciplined restlessness of the average class during a lesson in sight reading, a class taught by this phonics method is quiet, keenly interested, concentrating on learning and working. The difference is so great it must be seen to be believed.

And even if the logic of this natural approach to reading were less apparent, perhaps it would be necessary only to cite the extent of the English vocabulary to prove the point.

Otto Jespersen, the Danish philologist who made brilliant contributions to the study of phonetics, the English language and linguistics in general, conducted an investigation on this subject many years ago. He studied a group of college students and found that the majority possessed reading vocabularies of a little less than 60,000 words. Study of a cross-section of people who were high-school graduates and regular readers revealed average vocabularies of from 25,000 to 35,000 words.

Shakespeare used 21,000 different words in his writings and undoubt-edly understood another ten or twenty thousand words. In today's tech-nological world the average educated man may well need to know up-wards of 50,000 words. It is obvious that no one can begin to memorize the printed appearance of any such number. If, however, he has a basic grasp of phonics then each printed word automatically sounds in his mind at a glance. It speaks out to him instantly and clearly.

The reader of this book will wonder what controls and influences can have maintained erroneous teaching methods over the whole coun-try for thirty-odd years. Probably the chief causes lie in the extreme uni-formity of training in all American teachers' colleges as regards the three R's, and the many millions of dollars invested in the special readers which the sight method requires. Neither the publishers of these unique readers nor the schools themselves can lightly afford any change in this enormous market on the one hand and in their very heavy investment on the other. These factors, joined to the natural resistance of teachers to discarding what they have been taught and learning an entirely different method, are more powerful than the un-organized criticisms of parents. The methods whereby teachers are cer-tified in most states and the strength of their national organizations also tend to perpetuate existing uniform methodology in all teachers' col-leges. Another major factor has probably been the lack of an authorita-tive, tested, adequate and detailed teaching book on phonics.

But in recent years, the spontaneous and enthusiastic response to such books as Rudolf Flesch's WHY JOHNNY CAN'T READ (Harper & Brothers, New York, 1955) has been a clear indication of the con-cern of responsible American parents with the reading program in the schools. The fairest-minded among them have realized that other dele-terious factors are often at work—inadequate facilities, overcrowding, lack of trained and effective teachers, etc.—but their awareness that, even under the best available conditions, too many of their children fail to read well has resulted in the subjection of the sight method itself to the closest scrutiny.

The responses of the specialists in elementary education to the searching questions of the aroused public have been generally of two kinds, and both enlightening.

Some of the most vocal educators have cried out only against the temerity of those nonconformist teachers or laymen who had presumed to speak on the subject of teaching methods. Theirs is a defensive position, and in effect they deny that parents and public have a right, because of the technical complexities involved, to a full explanation of this comparative failure of the schools. The child who has not learned to read or write has not matured to the point of "reading readiness," they say. Or he may be emotionally unstable because of parental conflicts at home; he may receive too much or too little affection; or there may be other home conditions which promote insecurity. Perhaps he lacks proper discipline at home and must learn better behavior before he can read, or else they say his eyesight or hearing or general health or more often his intelligence may be defective.

However hackneyed these answers may seem to the parent disturbed by the failure of his child to read, it is important to realize that they are meant neither to obscure the issues nor to deceive. They are honest answers according to the lights of those who give them, a natural product of devotion to an educational theory so painstakingly developed through the years, so buttressed with formal courses of study for aspiring teachers, and so integrated with elaborate series of textbooks that it has become rather more an institution than it has remained a philosophy and a method. What the answers disclose is simply rigidity of thought in adhering to a technique that would be fine for a picture language—but English is an alphabetic one.

The other type of response to the widespread criticism of the day is, accordingly, the more heartening. There are many educators, in fact, who now openly admit that the sight method has not sufficed and that much of the material offered beginning readers is absurdly infantile. And the introduction of more or less phonics is gaining favor.

Yet, though phonics even at the third-grade level definitely does help, the application of this natural approach to reading is today fraught with confusion, even at the hands of the best-intentioned. Indeed, it is not unusual to hear the heads of curriculum of a city's public schools denounce phonics as destructive in some unexplained way of a child's grasp of the meaning of words, and at the same time require the teaching of some phonics throughout the system in the third grade and above. The difficulty here lies in the fact that so many children are so far behind and so frustrated after two or three years of failure that they do not quickly respond to *any* new method, especially if that method is the old-style, superficial phonics of thirty-five years ago, taught by a teacher who has never been taught a full system of phonics herself. It is in these situations that many educators otherwise responsive to the idea of change remain unwilling to abandon the sight method and defend that unwillingness by saying that some children learn better one way and some another, and that no one method of teaching is best for all.

This confusion constitutes, however, a definite breach in the anti-phonics wall—a breach which this book on the Unified Phonics Method is designed to expand, as a service to both teachers and parents who are seriously seeking to improve the language ability of our children. It is interesting that of the more than 400 teachers to whom I have taught this Unified method all have agreed that they had not known before that the English language was so directly phonetic and easy to teach.

CHAPTER II

The Remedy

IN HIS scholarly study, GROWTH AND STRUCTURE OF THE ENGLISH LANGUAGE,* Otto Jespersen said, "Whenever I think of the English language and compare it with others: it seems to me positively and expressly *masculine*, it is the language of a grown-up man and has very little childish or feminine about it. A great many things . . . confirm that impression, things phonetical, grammatical, and lexical. . . . First I shall mention the sound system. The English consonants are well defined . . . clearly and precisely pronounced." He quotes from another language by contrast to show that although full of music and harmony "the total impression is childlike and effeminate." He sums up the English language as methodical, energetic, businesslike, based on logical consistency but free from strict regulations of grammar or lexicon, and as having "an enormous richness of vocabulary."

Just how anyone can grasp the finer connotations of English words, or skillfully make use of the richness of its vocabulary, without first knowing thoroughly the phonetic basis of the language is hard to understand. In order to be known thoroughly, this phonetic basis should be acquired at one's first acquaintance with the printed word in the first school years, acquired so early that, a little later on, the

---

* 9th edition, Macmillan, New York, 1948.

sound of a printed word is mentally heard and recognized without re-sort to any distracting analysis of its component sounds. Such a pho-netic grasp of English is probably an absolute prerequisite for a poet, and even for a competent writer of English prose.

Even if merely a facility for reading with quick comprehension—not writing at all—were the only objective in teaching the language arts in school, the thorough and fundamental primary teaching of com-plete phonics appears to be the logical and uniformly effective means. It is perhaps the only practical way to learn to spell.

In the first place all nonpicture languages such as English—that is, those in which spoken sounds are conveyed in writing by certain sym-bols—are automatically and always phonetic languages. The symbols, which are letters or letter combinations, say certain definite sounds; that is their sole function. Accordingly, once anyone learns these sounds (about 45 in English), their symbols (about 70 letters or special letter combinations which we call phonograms), and the simple rules govern-ing their use, he can pronounce any written word correctly enough to recognize it if he knows that word when it is spoken.

It is this simple and readily learned instrument which phonics pro-vides, and with it completely at his command, almost any child can, by himself, learn to read anything written within the speaking vocabulary which he understands. This ability to read opens up to his eager imag-ination so many enthralling story books that from then on he seldom needs to be taught reading. He teaches himself. Very soon he recog-nizes at a glance, without recourse to his phonic knowledge, the short words and those which recur often. He soon reads such words by sight alone. He reserves his phonics knowledge for the printed words that are new to him, and he eventually comes to use it almost uncon-sciously, instantly, habitually. It does not impede his attention to the meaning of the word, or of the sentence. Instead it seems to eliminate any pondering or guessing at the word, thus simplifying and expedit-ing the continuity of his comprehension of the whole sentence.

In the nature of things every growing child first acquires a speaking vocabulary. He should then learn handwriting, and simultaneously he should be taught how to translate the spoken sounds into the written symbols (namely, the phonograms) which represent them. By assembling these symbols into words he can write ideas, and inversely he can read his own or the ideas of others. This was the sequence which the human race followed in building its alphabetic languages.

It is fundamental and logical that from the beginning the child should learn thoroughly the relation between the sounds of speech and their written symbols, for reading is not "guessing" at the meaning of words. It is not getting the meaning of a word by looking at an adjacent picture illustrating the word. It is not even pronouncing the sounds in sequence of the phonograms which constitute the spelling of the word. And reading is *not* getting the idea by having teacher tell what the word says. Reading is rather the process whereby the reader remembers those words he has often read before and mentally translates into sound the new words he encounters. He thereby instantly recognizes them, and their meaning falls into place among the other words he already knew. His mind then weighs the import of the sentence, for judgment is a vital part of reading.

Of course if a child is reading material which is too old for him he may pronounce the new words fairly well, but he won't understand. But any child understands many spoken words which he has not yet come to use in his conversation. It is these words which he must acquire the mental habit of deciphering by himself, using the phonics at his command, if he is really to learn them and become an easy, rapid and comprehending reader.

As I have already pointed out, however, much of the so-called phonics now being introduced piecemeal in many schools after one or two years or so of "whole word recognition" teaching, is superficial and incomplete—and has other serious shortcomings. For example it is a common practice to have the children pick out the short words which they can see in longer words—such as "and" in understand, or in candle, or "it" in critic or in habit, etc. This serves only to confuse, for these short "words" have no relation whatever to the meaning of the words in which they can be "discovered."

Another fallacy in this pseudo-phonics teaching is the idea that the child should learn "families" of words—that is, words which are spelled and sound alike, except for one or two letters. Such words in the all family are ball, call, fall, tall, hall, etc. Meaning is the important factor in reading but the meanings of these "family" words are utterly foreign to each other. In fact, this similarity in appearance well illustrates one reason why reading by "remembering the appearance" of a word—that is, by whole word recognition—is so unsound and so difficult unless a child has had a thorough grounding in phonics.

The more advanced schools, it is true, no longer use the confusing "word game" or the "word family" teaching devices. Along with his basic training in sight reading, many of them teach the child the sounds of most single-letter consonants, late in his first grade. In the second grade some of the vowel sounds and a few two-letter phonograms are taught. More are added, together with a few spelling rules, during each of the next four grades. In such schools the child entering seventh grade may have been taught much of the phonics which he could and ought to learn in the first grade, but he will have had very little practice and hence very little ability to use it. His habit of mind toward reading and spelling will still be the whole-word memorizing and the guessing from context or pictures of the "sight" reader. His mind does not "hear" the word at a glance, nor can he even readily analyze its component sounds because he has never been trained in this technique. At best he has learned only that such a technique is possible for many words.

The common misunderstanding about the phonetic basis of English and how it should be taught accounts for the claim that phonics teaching tends to block a child's easy comprehension in reading. In fact it appears that scientific and true phonics teaching eliminates the blocking of the reader's comprehension. When he must otherwise search his memory to recall the word by its overall appearance or, that failing, must just guess at it, then he does tend to lose the meaning of the sentence. If each difficult word is accompanied by an illustrative cartoon he gets a rough idea of what the word says from the picture. But that is not reading English. It is more like puzzling through a "comic" strip.

The Unified Phonics Method is distinctly different and it supplies what has been lacking heretofore—a simple, workable and thorough method for teaching phonics in the home or in the classroom. This method differs basically from other phonic methods in that it does not start with reading, which is, in phonics, the translating of printed letters or words into the sounds of spoken words. Instead it first teaches the child the *writing* of the sounds by using the letters which say the sounds. This direct approach from the *sounds* of the words the child knows and uses in speaking into the *written characters* which represent the sounds is a direct, simple, logical explanation to him of the whole writing and reading process. He is not bewildered by this new world of letters. He grasps the idea almost at once. He is delighted to find that he can use the twenty-six letters of the alphabet to say on paper the many words he speaks. In other words, he learns to spell. As soon as he can write a word he can usually read it, often at a glance wherever he sees it. In fact, reading as such need not be taught to many children, but training in the *blending* of the sounds in a syllable is needed for some. When a child has once mastered the phonic tools, he is able to decipher and pronounce and understand any printed words which come within his speaking vocabulary. Not only does he comprehend those words but also the many others which he hears and understands, but has not as yet come to use.

The fact that this method teaches spelling first, by actually writing the sounds of words on paper, is believed to be a complete departure from other phonics teaching methods, and a distinct advance. The other major contribution is the completeness of its phonetics, and its simplicity. There is a reason or rule to cover *almost* every spelling in English. A study of word formation and euphony has contributed to formulating a set of easily learned, simple rules which explain and govern the spelling of all words suitable to each school grade, with surprisingly few, and easily learned, exceptions.

I have called this system of teaching the language subjects the Unified Phonics Method because it is based on showing and teaching the constant connection between the sounds of the spoken language and the characters which represent them in the written language. Speaking, writing, spelling and reading are taught as related parts of a single subject—the English language—and the method follows the same natural teaching sequence by which man developed language itself. Furthermore it is based on the physical and neurological processes of the human brain. It is also carefully designed to prevent the typical errors which children make in speech, spelling and reading. In a word it is a scientifiic method of teaching language.

All of us do use word recognition in reading. We must acquire it, and after learning phonics we do so almost automatically, often without any teaching or training, and in accordance with the acuity of our individual visual memories. Sight reading or recognition of words at a glance requires no teaching for a child who knows phonics. Common and familiar words are soon recognized and read at sight with easy sentence comprehension *provided* the tool of phonics is at hand to identify any new or less familiar words. However it has been found to be very confusing to the great majority of first- or second-grade children who are taught this method if any form of whole word recognition, or sight method of teaching is introduced.

These are the children who are not born with "unilateral dominance" for reading, but have to acquire it. Unilateral dominance is an inherited physical characteristic which has no relation to intelligence. It is, in effect, as Dr. Orton demonstrated, the mental habit of always using the same side of the brain to receive and retain the image of printed letters in words for the purpose of fixing meaning to them. This habit results in the image always showing in one direction. However, most children inherit more or less of a tendency to use either side of the brain, a tendency which results in their sometimes receiving the image of the letters in reverse, or more often in the image being confused. These latter children comprise at least half of any group, and usually three-fourths of the boys. The extent of their resultant reading disability varies all the way from an easily corrected degree for some children to a complete disability for others when any sight reading is attempted.

The Unified Phonics Method of teaching enables every child in a group to acquire the unilateral dominance necessary for reading without delaying or disturbing the progress of those fortunate few who are born with it. As in the teaching of any subject, some children need much more time and attention than others. This area of unilateral dominance is, indeed, one where parents can be of enormous help because they can learn and teach the Unified Phonics Method at home without interfering with, but actually supplementing and reinforcing the classroom teaching.

It seems essential, in fact, that parents as well as teachers should know and understand the methods of teaching the language arts to children. Education cannot be confined to the classroom. Most children want to be shown how to write and to read long before they reach school age. There is every reason why they should be taught as many of the preliminary steps at home as they can master, provided the right method is used.

Parents must realize also that schools cannot easily change their method of teaching, and individual teachers usually have little latitude in this respect. Very many children cannot progress in language except by means of a sound use of phonics, but even those teachers who know this are not free in many schools to change from the method in vogue. However, there is no reason why a mother or father cannot teach this Unified Phonics Method at home. Such teaching will greatly help most children to keep up with their class. Any child can use this training in school regardless of his inability to memorize whole words as may be required of him in class. It cannot obstruct or interfere with the method of teaching which is in use at school. Most teachers will agree with this, although it is not uncommon for teachers to say that they prefer that children shall not be helped at home.

The lessons and teaching techniques in the following chapters are, therefore, intended for parents and teachers who are interested in advancing the writing, spelling and reading of their children beyond the unduly low standards that are the presently accepted American norms for the different grades.

But before proceeding to the detailed discussion of lessons and teaching techniques, I think it pertinent to describe rather fully the successful results achieved with this method in practice, results to which I alluded in the *Introduction*. Let me first tell about teaching the non-readers—those with severe reading disability.

I have been privileged to enjoy a remarkably rewarding experience in giving individual one-hour lessons with this method to more than three hundred children with severe reading and spelling disabilities during the last twenty years in Bronxville, N.Y., Cambridge and Honolulu. All of them were bright, intelligent children who were, nevertheless, from one to six years below the American standard in language for their school age. Many had already repeated a whole year with no real improvement in reading. They are typical of the very many children who can learn to read acceptably only by this one method. Without this help they become frustrated and hopeless. As a result they often become problem children. This fact has perhaps been the mainspring behind my many years of study and work in this neglected field.

All of these children had been taught by the sight method and about half had had special remedial teaching by that method or by incomplete phonics. It was necessary to break down their wrong habits and their defeatism and resistance to thinking—that is, to working at spelling, writing and reading. Nevertheless, all these children who completed a full course with me were brought up to grade in these subjects. There have been few instances where neither the mother nor teacher cooperated with me to help a child. Such help is necessary for severe cases of reading disability. Many of these children were referred to me by family doctors, chiefly pediatricians, who saw that their behavior problems resulted largely from frustration in reading at school. Doctors, of course, are more aware of the unilateral dominance factor in regard to language ability, and educators generally are not.

Now let me give some results attained in classroom teaching.

The superintendent of a system of twenty-four large private schools in Hawaii was so impressed by the phenomenally rapid improvement of many children I taught that he asked me about four years ago to teach the Unified Phonics Method to a group of his elementary teachers. First I gave sixty teachers a two weeks' course for an hour and a half each day after school, and I followed this up with a more thorough six weeks' course of thirty hours in the summer. The school superintendent then requested fourteen teachers to volunteer to follow this method strictly and exclusively in teaching the language subjects. All the classes were exceptionally large, averaging fifty-one pupils. Seventeen other teachers in nine of this system's schools who had had no instruction in the Unified Phonics Method were told to continue their usual teaching by the whole word recognition method or any phonics method they had been using. These were the control groups. All these teachers were asked to keep accurate records and to give the standard Metropolitan Achievement Tests for their grades.

So striking were the results that many more teachers asked to be instructed the following summer. Within a year and a half the gains by the classes taught under the Unified Phonics Method proved so outstanding that the entire school system, comprising some fifteen thousand children, adopted this method officially. All teachers in the first, second and third grades were asked to complete a thirty-hour course of training under me before September 1955, and to teach this method exclusively. In mid-October of that year a conference of about sixty of these teachers was held. Their enthusiasm over their classroom results was most rewarding and exciting.

The success of the teachers and of the children with this method can be seen from the tests given, and I only regret I cannot also show the wonderful "working spirit" in the classes.

Standard Metropolitan Achievement Tests given to six *first*-grade classes after eight months in school show the following average accomplishment for all these children. Their average median reading score was 11½ months higher than the average score of all *first*-grade children in American schools. That is, they were reading as well as the average American child is doing in the early months of the *third* grade. There is no spelling standard for the first grade, so spelling tests were not given.

Nine *second*-grade classes made an average median reading score 6.9 months above the American norm for their grade, and their spelling scores were an average of 19½ months above the American norm.

Nine *third*-grade classes made an average reading score only ¼ month above the norm, and an average spelling score 6 months better than the norm.

Four *fourth*-grade classes scored ¼ month above the American norm in reading and 11 months above in spelling.

One *sixth*-grade class in 8 months advanced 14 months in reading and 26 months in spelling. The other *sixth* grade started the method in October 1954 with average scores 7 months below the U.S. norms, but by May 1955 it was up to the U.S. norm, with reading and spelling 8 months ahead.

One *seventh*-grade class scored 3 months ahead of the U.S. norm in reading, 15 months ahead in spelling and 6 months ahead in English.

The first year's experiment evidenced the very real advantage of this teaching method. These classes in the 3rd, 4th, 6th and 7th grades actually made great gains during the year, for they all started with scores far below the norm as a result of their prior years in school under other methods of teaching reading and spelling. In fact they had to "unlearn" faulty habits acquired before.

The gains in all grades despite such very large classes are the more remarkable in that these teachers had had little or no prior experience in teaching by this method.

The report of the chairman of the teachers' committee in charge of this 1954 experiment reads in part as follows:

It became immediately apparent that previous to the experiment a large number of children had not been making a year's advancement within a year's time. Somewhere there had been a leakage. Secondly it was noted that the first grades taught by the Spalding Method scored higher class medians than those which were not. Moreover, in the Spalding classes the number of children more than a year above grade level was astonishingly high while there were exceedingly few failures.

These were teachers of twenty years' experience, highly esteemed in the teaching profession. In their second year of using the Spalding Method they had even better results. None of these teachers would return to the sight reading method or even another "phonetic" method.

What was the picture in the third grade? Classes taught by the sight reading method or even other phonic methods in first or second grades were usually below the grade norm for beginning third grade. After a year of the Spalding Method they picked up and ended the year above grade norm in nearly all subjects.

The children in fifth, sixth, and seventh grades made remarkable progress and were able to reach and surpass their grade norm in nearly all subjects but with tremendous effort owing to their delayed start. Before progress could begin, much had to be undone. Ingrained guessing habits had to be broken; inattentiveness as a defence mechanism had to be overcome before those experiencing difficulty could be helped. The method became remedial in the upper grades. The graphs depicting their progress resemble Gothic cathedrals.

The lowest marks in the fifth, sixth, and seventh grades occurred in history, geography, and literature. This is understandable since a high mark in these subjects in an achievement test presupposes a wide reading knowledge over a fairly long period of time. If a child has been handicapped in reading, it will take time for him to catch up in these subjects. In arithmetic, spelling, and English progress will be almost immediate.

As we mentioned, one reason for continuing the experiment was to see if the children's progress would continue or reach a leveling off point. It continued, the gains of the second year in nearly all cases equaling or surpassing the first.

But to return to the subject of the first grade. These children startled everyone. They grasped the 70 phonograms, were able to apply them, and they became independent readers, speakers, and writers. The so-called slow learners became self-reliant in the same way the quick learners did though they had to work harder and achieved a goal somewhat lower. The point is that they did achieve their goal. They did do their work. They were promoted because they had completed the first grade work. They were not automatically promoted to the second grade where they might continue to do first grade work in a separate group. If the child who has difficulty knows the sounds, despite his poor visual recall he can pronounce the word and arrive at the meaning through auditory recall. Normally the word will be a part of the child's hearing vocabulary. What was known through one sense is now common knowledge of both senses through correlation of both sight and hearing. This method of word recognition directs the child in the use of his total sensory process. The child thus becomes master of the learning process becoming gradually independent of the teacher and her techniques. The children who experienced no difficulty soared in their other subjects and achieved maximum success because they were given the opportunity to do so.

Because of the odium attached to the word "phonics" in many minds and also because the Spalding Method is much more than mere phonics used in the popular sense, I hesitate to use that word in discussing the work done in the schools of Honolulu. There is no other phonics course that I know of which attempts to teach a first grader or even an older child every single sound (and that includes silent letters of course) in every word. In others sounds are taught but in such an erratic and isolated fashion, and so slowly over a period of years, that the child is constantly encountering unknown portions of words which he must necessarily guess or be told. This procedure is labeled "intelligent guessing." Whether or not it is intelligent to guess words when reading, can be seen in the fruits of the reading. Guessing is not tolerated in any other subject. As adults we are even penalized in certain tests for taking a guess at an answer. We are intolerant of methods of teaching arithmetic which encourage guessing the tables or the combinations. A thinker forges his way to the truth. He does not guess it.

What children profit most from the Spalding method? Every one does, according to his mental gifts. The progress of every fifth child in all classes participating in the testing program was charted. The top child gained three or four years in nine months in many cases.

Some of the comparative results are tabulated below.

First Grade

METROPOLITAN ACHIEVEMENT TESTS IN MAY	WORD MEANING				AVERAGE READING		AVERAGE ACHIEVEMENT			
	Experiment Class		Control Class		Experiment Class		Experiment Class		Control Class	
	Number of Children	Percentage	Number of Children	Percentage	Number of Children	Percentage	Number of Children	Percentage	Number of Children	Percentage
More than one Year above Grade Level	264	71%	98	30%	252	68%	217	59%	74	23%
At and up to a year above Grade Level	88	24%	155	47%	102	28%	135	36%	227	69%
Below Grade Level	19	5%	75	23%	15	4%	17	5%	27	8%
	369		328		369		369		328	

The Superintendent of these 24 schools in Hawaii expressed his attitude toward this course in a recent March 21, 1956 bulletin to the Administrative Council and teachers: "Our prime purpose in the elementary schools is to teach children to think, to develop the intellectual virtues. Reading is fundamental to this growth and development. The phonics program is absolutely necessary if we expect to achieve maximum success with the whole group."

I think it significant, in refutation of the criticism sometimes made about all phonics teaching, that the most able readers in these large classes have made such spectacular advances while their less competent classmates have just about come up to the normal grade.

Recent *Morrison-McCall Spelling Tests* in classes where children have now been taught by this method for about two years show some interesting results. The teachers are satisfied that their reading is about as well advanced as their spelling. The teachers are all delighted and find their second year's work with this method is much easier for them.

These recent February 1956 spelling tests in five first-grade classes with 268 children showed a median score of 3.2. This means that their spelling is up to the American standard for the second month in the third grade. Only 6 children in all the 268 scored below the norm for their grade. Three of the five classes had no child below grade.

Four classes in second grade with 208 children made an average median score of 4.2 or 16 months ahead of the standard American norm for their grade.

Two *third*-grade classes of 59 and 61 children each made average spelling scores of 6.0, which is the standard score for beginning sixth grade. The lowest child's score in one class was 3.3 and in the other 3.5. Only two other children were below the norm for their grade of 3.6. No other test scores are available at this writing but there is no indication that these results are in any way misleading. They all point toward the complete elimination of "remedial" reading. These schools have had no special or remedial teachers, a considerable cash saving as well as a great saving of children.

The teachers whose results are recorded here are, to be sure, highly competent and devoted. It is inspiring to talk with them and see their enthusiasm for this method of teaching the language arts. Two of them spent their summer teaching this method to groups of some 240 teachers in Boston. So far I have given this course to 323 public school teachers and to 290 private school teachers. Many others have requested similar courses.

There are grounds for belief, then, that this book is needed.

There cannot be very much wrong with a teaching method which works so exceptionally well that in such large classes even the poorest scholar does not do badly.

The proof of any method of teaching lies not in the academic theories concerning it, nor in the "research" work conducted usually to prove or disprove a theory, but rather in the actual daily and yearly results of its use. There is no argument that can stand against such facts, no matter how learned, prominent and respected may be the educator who presents it. My confidence in this method in the hands of any conscientious teacher rests on the fact that it always produces results which other methods do not appear even to approach.

CHAPTER III

Fundamentals in Teaching Phonics

THE WRITTEN or printed language should be presented to a beginner as a series of symbols each of which represents one of the component sounds of a spoken word. This is fundamental. It ties together logically the written and the spoken word. Speaking, writing and reading are thus understood and taught as related. This is the only reasoned approach to any alphabetic language.

There are 70 common phonograms in English. They are the single letters or letter combinations which represent 45 *basic* sounds used in the spoken language. (The phonograms are listed at the end of this chapter.) The first step in reading and spelling is to learn these phonograms so well that in any printed word they stand out clearly *as a series of sounds,* and not merely as a series of letters.

The short and common words soon come to be recognized automatically as representing ideas, without the need of separating them into their component phonograms for reading. Writing at first requires such analysis to get the spelling right. For spelling, new words should always be studied by their phonetic sounds from the *spoken* word. True spelling is writing from the spoken word.

I have found that it is a mistake to place spelling books in the hands of the children. "Spelling" books are not good for teaching

38

spelling because they do not help to relate the spelling to the sounds of the words. If the child looks at printed words and merely copies them, he learns only by memory and without reasoning. Few spelling books tell the child to translate any of the letters into their corresponding sounds. They make him depend almost wholly on his visual recall. This is a real handicap to most if not to all children. I repeat, true spelling is translating *speech* into written symbols.

Most spelling books now introduce new words in whole sentences or paragraphs, but that makes it a reading, not a spelling, lesson.

In teaching spelling by the Unified Phonics Method new words are dictated by the teacher and written by the children from her verbal dictation. Any troublesome words are discussed from the point of view of the symbols which represent the sounds. The spelling is first reasoned, then memorized. The meaning is of course discussed. "Word" connotes meaning. A word is the smallest unit of speech which by itself has any meaning. The children give oral sentences containing the new word. Then, assuming he has a sufficient vocabulary, each child writes *his own* original sentence containing it. This teaches true *spelling* in the spelling lesson.

Two-thirds of the phonograms have only one sound. Eleven have two sounds and ten have three sounds. In addition to learning the phonograms, and applying them, there are a few laws of spelling which must be learned and used. All of them are summarized at the end of Chapter V.

The above may seem like a difficult project for a six-year-old; actually it is not. He learns both the phonograms and the laws rapidly and easily. They are simple and logical statements. The mental capacity of a six-year-old is not to be underestimated nor should his desire to learn be unrecognized.

Keeping this in mind, the teacher will see the importance of following exactly certain general procedures in her work. I have evolved these procedures by the most careful trial and testing over many years. These procedures, with neither additions nor deletions, I have found to be the most effective for successful results with all children.

First and foremost, the parent and teacher should elicit the intelligent and enthusiastic interest of the child in learning the written language. And this can only be done well by opening the door for him to the basis and meaning of writing—namely, that the letters stand for the sounds he makes when he says a word. Take any purely phonetic word, divide it verbally and in writing into syllables, and then divide the syllables into the phonetic sounds of each letter. Have him repeat the separate letter sounds (not their names), the syllables and the word. Tell him the letters *are* these sounds, not that they are merely symbolic of the sounds. And then explain that this is all there is to the written and printed words. Tell him you will teach him the sounds of the letters and how to write them, and that he can then write words and can say the words which others have written (or printed in books). This prospect is enough to excite the keenest interest of a child. The teaching procedures given below will maintain that same interest in the language subjects throughout his elementary school years.

One. Teach the phonograms by having the pupils say in unison the one or more sounds of each phonogram, showing them one phonogram card after another in varying sequences. Correct handwriting is taught from the very start, practicing only with the phonograms. Have them write on paper each phonogram just *after* they pronounce it. This unites the visual, aural and kinesthetic functions of the brain. The child sees, hears, says, writes and feels the symbol, and thus learns it. He is made aware of just how he makes the precise sounds, and of how he forms the related symbols for each phonogram.

Two. Avoid naming the letters. Use their phonetic sounds instead. The child should come to *think* of the letters as being sounds. (In English words, only five (ā, ē, ī, ō, ū) of the twenty-six letters *ever* use the sound of their names, and these five letters more often say ă, ě, ĭ, ŏ, ŭ). It is easier to unify speech, writing and reading by not injecting the names of letters. This simplifies the learning of the language. (Of course, before the third grade the children should know the name by which we designate the letter when talking of it, but the teaching time for spelling in all grades should be spent learning its sounds rather than its name.)

Three. Always call the phonogram containing two or more letters by its sound; that is to say, never spell it out. For example, eigh has one sound. "Neighbor" contains four phonograms and "naval" contains five; the first five letters in "neighbor" have the same two sounds as the first two in "naval." The child should be taught to identify every phonogram in a word readily, and to think habitually of each as a distinct sound, whether it is a one-letter or a four-letter phonogram.

Four. Teach and require accurate pronunciation and correct, legible handwriting from the very beginning.

Five. As soon as the phonograms are fairly well learned, dictate words from the Ayres list for the children to write, making sure that they say aloud each phonogram of a one-syllable word and *each syllable* of longer words *just before* they start to write it. The children are not to see these words on the board or elsewhere, until they write them.

Six. Teach the basic laws (and exceptions) for spelling as they come up in writing words. The pupils should learn to use them by repeating the applicable spelling laws in every new word they write, until each child knows *and* uses them.

Seven. Where no rule governs the choice of which phonogram to use to represent a certain sound in a word, it can only be learned by memory, and the dictionary is referred to as the only authority. (We are not inventing a language; we are learning to understand and use the one we have.)

Eight. Remember that the real study of the language—the time when the pupils and teacher analyze the connection between the sound of a spoken word and its written symbols—is in the spelling period. Spelling is the basic key to a grasp of the written language and, for that matter, of the spoken one.

Nine. Reading from a book is not begun until the pupils have completely learned (just as outlined in the above procedures) enough common words to comprehend instantly the meaning of a sentence.

The phonograms are printed on the following pages. In teaching it is very convenient to use seventy separate cards which display the phonograms in type large enough to be seen across the room. The cards have the key sounds in smaller type printed on the back only for the teacher's information. The child learns only the sounds and the writing of them. Prove to him that these sounds are in the words he says, but never teach the sounds by the use of key words.

It is important to follow all the teaching notes, the sequences, and the instructions given in this book. If this is done it is confidently predicted that a conscientious teacher will have no normally intelligent child in her group below the national median level. Indeed, the median for the group should soon be about two years beyond the present national average in both reading and spelling, as well as in handwriting and speech.

Before teaching the sounds it is advisable to check and correct one's pronunciation of the phonograms. For example the sound of *l* is not "el" but only that of the last letter, the sound "b" is not "bŭh," and "k" is not "cŭh." We do not say robŭ but only rob. Segregate the phonogram sounds in the key words as a check on the correct sounds.

The 70 phonograms which follow were worked out by a group of language teachers under Dr. Samuel T. Orton's direction. These are printed as separate cards with key words to show their one or more sounds printed on the reverse side of each just as shown here.

* Sets of the phonogram cards are available. For information and prices write to Whiteside, Inc., 425 Fourth Ave., New York 16, N. Y.

b	f
c	g
d	h

44

4

f

if

1

b

rib

5

g

"g"   bag

"j"   gem

g can say "j" only when followed by e, i or y. Thus the sound of this letter can be readily determined and no number is needed to indicate the use of the second sound.

2

c

"k"   can

"s"   cent

c followed by e, i or y says "s." Followed by any other letter it says "k." Thus the sound of this letter can be told at a glance so no number is needed to indicate the second sound.

6

h

him

3

d

lid

j

m

k

n

l

p

10

m

am

7

i

jam

11

n

in

8

k

ink

12

p

map

9

l

lag

"l" is sounded with the tongue point pressed against the roof of the mouth.

qu	t
r	v
s	w

16

t

bat

13

qu

"kw" quit

This sound is always written with two letters. The u is not a vowel here.

17

v

viv id

The teeth are placed on the lower lip at the same place for "f" as for "v." In writing many children confuse these two sounds unless they are taught to hear and feel the differences.

14

r

rat

"r" is sounded with the tongue point at the roof of the mouth. "r" is not "er."

18

w

wit

Round the lips to say "w." The sound is not "wŭ."

15

s

"s" us

"z" as²

x	a
y	e
z	i

22

a

"ă" at

"ā" na̱ vy

"ah" wȧnt

19

x

"ks" box

In "tacks" the "k" is a separate sound from the "s." Sound the "ks" of x as one sound.

23

e

"ĕ" end

"ē" me̱

20

y

yet

This consonant letter y is used only at the beginning of a syllable, usually the first one.

"ĭ" ba̱ by

"ī" my̱

24

i

"ĭ" In di an

"ī" si̱ lent

Both i's in Indian say "ĭ." i and y at the end of a syllable usually say "ĭ." The other vowels should say their names at the end of a syllable.

21

z

zest

o	ir
u	ur
er	wor

52

28

ir

f**ir**st

Her first nurse works early.

29

ur

n**urse**₌⁵

Her first nurse works early.

30

wor

w**or**ks

Her first nurse works early.

(wor is made of two phonograms.
or may say "er" when w comes before it.)

25

o

"ŏ"   odd

"ō"   o̱ pen

"o̅o̅"   do̊³

26

u

"ŭ"   up

"ū"   mu̱ s̆ic²

"ŏŏ"   půt³

27

er

h**er**

Her first nurse works early.

This sentence gives five spellings
for the sound "er."

ear	th
sh	ay
ee	ai

34 **th** "th" <u>th</u>in (Breath hisses between tongue-tip and upper teeth) "~~th~~" ²<u>th</u>is (Tongue position is same as above but the voice gives sound as air is forced out)	**31** **ear** **<u>ear</u> ly** H<u>er</u> f<u>ir</u>st n<u>ur</u>se w<u>or</u>ks <u>ear</u>ly.
35 **ay** "ā" d<u>ay</u>	**32** **sh** di<u>sh</u> sh is used at the beginning of a word, at the end of a syllable, but not at the beginning of a syllable after the first one.
36 **ai** "ā" p<u>ai</u>nt	**33** **ee** "ē" s<u>ee</u>

ow	oi
ou	aw
oy	au

40 oi p<u>oi</u>nt	**37** ow "ow" h<u>ow</u> "ō" l<u>ow</u>²
41 aw l<u>aw</u>	**38** ou "ow" r<u>ou</u>nd "ō" f<u>ou</u>²r "ōō" y<u>ou</u>³ "ŭ" c<u>ou</u>⁴n try
42 au f<u>au</u>lt	**39** oy b<u>oy</u>

ew	ch
ui	ng
oo	ea

46	**43**

46

ch

"ch" mu<u>ch</u>

"k" s<u>ch</u>ool²

"sh" <u>ch</u>iv al ry³

43

ew

"o͞o" gr<u>ew</u>

"ū" n<u>ew</u>²

(Same sounds as for ui.)

47

ng

ra<u>ng</u>

(ng is a nasal sound. It is neither "n" nor "g" nor is it a combination of them.)

44

ui

"o͞o" fr<u>ui</u>t

"ū" s<u>ui</u>t²

(Same sounds as for ew.)

48

ea

"ē" <u>ea</u>t

"ĕ" h<u>ea</u>d²

"ā" br<u>ea</u>k³

45

oo

"o͞o" b<u>oo</u>t

"o͝o" f<u>oo</u>t²

"ō" fl<u>oo</u>r³

ar	**or**
ck	**wh**
ed	**oa**

52

or

o<u>r</u>

49

ar

f<u>ar</u>

53

wh

"hw"   <u>wh</u>en

h is a breathing sound and therefore h + w is not the same
sound as w alone.

50

ck

ne<u>ck</u>

(Used only after a single vowel
which does not say its name.)

54

oa

b<u>oa</u>t

51

ed

"ĕd"   grad <u>ed</u>

"d"   lov<u>e</u>d²

"t"   <u>wreck</u>ed³

This card is the past tense ending—not the "ĕ" and "d" of red.

ey	igh
ei	eigh
ie	kn

58

igh

"ī"   sigh

55

ey

"ā"   they[2]

"ē"   key[2]

"ĭ"   val ley[3]

59

eigh

"ā"   weigh

56

ei

"ē"   con ceit

"ā"   veil[2]

"ĭ"   for feit[3]

See page 3 in the notebook for the rule for the use of ei and ie.

60

kn

"n"   knot

Used only at the beginning of a base word.

57

ie

"ē"   field

"ī"   pie[2]

"ĭ"   lil ies[3][2]

See page 3 in the notebook for the rule for the use of ie and ei.

gn

dge

wr

oe

ph

gh

64	**61**
dge	**gn**
"ĭ" bridge	"n" gnat
May be used only after a single vowel which does not say its name.	Used both at the beginning and at the end of a base word. (reign)
65	**62**
oe	**wr**
"ō" toe	"r" wrap
	There is no sound of w here.
66	**63**
gh	**ph**
"g" ghost	"f" phan tom

ti

ough

si

ci

70

ough

"ō" though[2]

"ōō" through[2]

"ŭf" rough[3]

"ŏf" cough[4]

"aw" thought[5]

"ow" bough[6]

67

ti

"sh" na tion

ti, si, ci say "sh" when they are together for the sound. See page 4 in the notebook.

68

si

"sh" ses sion

"zh" vi sion[2]

ti, si, ci say "sh."
si is the only one which can say "zh." See page 4 in the notebook.

69

ci

"sh" fa cial

ti, si, ci say "sh." See page 4 in the notebook.

CHAPTER IV

Handwriting

THE TEACHING of writing should precede reading. This is fundamental. It is the only approach to the printed or written language
that is clear and understandable to all children. Writing brings into
play the kinesthetic controls, that is, the use of the hand muscles,
which are coordinated with those of the mouth when the child pro-
nounces the sound of each phonogram before he writes it. Most children have some confusion in the proper sequence of letters in words
for both reading and spelling, and this method overcomes such confusion. I follow a definite, detailed teaching pattern to prevent the
numerous mistakes which otherwise are made so frequently that wrong
habits are soon acquired.

I should like to say at this point that good and facile handwriting is a most important part of language. The lack of it is a constant
handicap. It can be quickly acquired only if correct and exact techniques are well taught from the start, and well maintained at all times.
The sounds of the phonograms are learned at the same time.

The Sounds and Formation of the Twenty-six Letters

Introduce handwriting by showing the class the printed twenty-
six single-letter phonograms on the cards, saying all the sounds of each
phonogram. Write each one in manuscript writing on the blackboard.

Before long you will do this while the children write it, just after they have repeated its sound. This familiarizes them with both the printed and written forms and their English sounds. No particular order or sequence is desirable after the first lesson.

Introduce all the lower case letters in the first lesson, if possible.

A few rules to guide a child in forming and placing the letters are a great help. The children are familiar with the clock face, and it is therefore useful in teaching how the letters are formed. Since the numbers on the clock are always in the same position, this makes an easy reference guide for children.

Many teachers fail to realize the importance of teaching the correct formation of the letters from the very start of teaching the written language. Unless children write correctly they do not *see* the correct symbols for the sounds. The best time to stop wrong habits is before they begin.

The size and spacing of letters is important. For this reason the standard ruled paper where the lines are ⅜ths of an inch apart can be used from the beginning.

Every third line will be the base line for beginners in the first grade (or for beginners in handwriting at any grade), because at first children cannot easily form letters as small as those in normal adult writing. It is well for them to put a little pencil mark on the beginning of every third line of ruled paper so that they will know which lines to use as base lines. They should write the short letters to *fill* the space between the base line and the line above (⅜″ high), and the tall letters go to the second line above the base line.

Position for Both Left-handed and Right-handed Children

Sit with hips against the back of the chair.

Put both feet on the floor but put no pressure on them, nor in the knees.

Sit with the head pushed up as high as possible so as to have *no* weight on the arms as they rest on the desk.

Tip the body forward but keep it about two inches away from the desk.

Put both forearms on the desk, with elbows just off the front edge of the desk.

Keep the side of the paper parallel to the writing arm. (Like a railroad track, the arm is one track and the edge of the paper is the other.)

The left-handed child needs special attention. Be sure that he holds the side of his paper parallel to his writing arm. A strip of Scotch Tape pasted near the top of his desk to show the slanting direction to which the top edge of his paper should be parallel is a very useful aid to him. It keeps him from turning his paper like that of his right-handed neighbors. He should be watched to see that his writing hand is always below the base line on which he writes. He should also be told from the first that his letters can all be straight up and down or that he can use a slant provided the slant is backhand, and never forward. The forward slant, for a lefthanded writer, forces his hand into a most awkward, and hence wrong position.

The use of the hand which does not write is very important. It does the same work as a roller on a typewriter, i.e., it always *holds* the paper in position, and *moves it* back and forth and up and down on the desk so that the writing arm need never move up or down. The elbow of the writing arm like the hinge of the typewriter type bar (which puts the letter on the paper) has a fixed position.

The writing hand rests and slides on the ball of the palm and on the side of the little finger below the end joint. (This keeps the little finger from curling under too far and acting as a brake that prevents the hand from sliding easily across the paper. A mention of the way the brake on the bicycle stops the bicycle, helps the child feel what you are saying.)

How to Hold a Pencil

Hold the pencil between the thumb and the third finger. They are held opposite each other to form a vise. Round the index finger

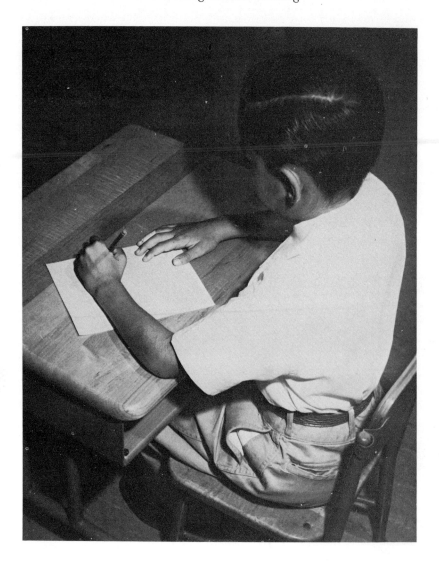

Correct writing position for left-handed child.

Correct writing position for right-handed child.

and avoid pinching the pencil. Hold it at the place where the paint begins—about an inch from the point. The pencil should lie on the index finger just below the knuckle. This places the point of the pencil in the best position for writing. The sketches that follow are intended to illustrate this important matter to both teacher and pupil.

Keep the wrist flat (*not resting on the side!*) Make sure there is *no pressure* on the writing hand or arm. Teachers of little children ask them to make their arms and hands feel as light and soft as the leg and paw of a friendly kitten feels.

Position at the Blackboard

Stand about 18 inches away, no closer, and write at the eye level.

Curl fingers slightly. Lay the four fingers along the length of the chalk. The thumb is on the opposite side. This permits the use of the *side* of the point for writing.

These sketches show how the pencil is held in the right hand.

The pencil is held this way in the left hand.

Detailed Techniques of Teaching
the Lower-case Manuscript Letters

The teacher gives the general rules governing the letters.

All letters sit on the line.

Letters are of two sizes only. They are either *tall* or *short*. Tall letters reach two-thirds the way up to the base line above. Short letters are half as tall as tall letters. They occupy one-third of the space between the base lines. However beginners will at first make the letters three times larger, as stated before. This large size is used in the following directions.

Manuscript letters are made up of parts of the clock, and straight lines. The teacher's blackboard presentation should show this:

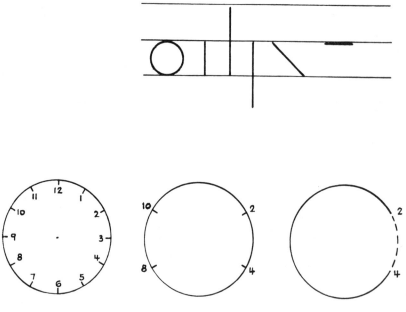

| The Clock Face | These are the four points we use most often | This shows how we use the clock to write c (from 2 to 4) |

Presentation of Letters that Begin at 2 on the Clock
Method: Teacher, holding up card a, says the three sounds: "ă, ā, ah" (Say them in a staccato manner, not run together).

Teacher: "I will show you how this letter is written. It is a short letter. Short letters fill the space from the base line to the line above. Start far enough in from the edge of your paper to make a circle, which looks like the clock-face. Start at 2, go up and all the way around the clock to 2 again; from there pull a line straight down to the base line and leave it."

The class says the three sounds for a and each child writes a on his paper.

Teacher then holds up card c and says the two sounds: "k, s."

The class repeats the two sounds of c.

This is a short letter. Start just far enough from a to make a clock. Begin at 2 and go up and around the clock and stop at 4.

Teacher holds up card d and gives its sound, "d."

Help the children to see that the round part comes first. Get each child to feel his tongue making a circle within his mouth as he says "d." (b begins with a line and in saying "b" the lips make a straight line. The kinesthetic feel of these two letters can keep children from reversing them. "d" begins with a circle and "b" begins with a straight line.)

Start at 2 to make the short round part, go up and all the way around the clock, go straight up to the second line above, pull a line straight down to the base line, and leave it.

Teacher shows card f and gives its sound "f." The children repeat the sound.

f is a tall letter. It starts below the second line above at 2. Go around the top to 10 (or "round it" to 10), pull straight down to the base line. Put on a little cross in the direction in which we write.

Class repeats the two sounds of g: "g, j."
This short letter starts at 2. Go up and all the way around the clock. Close it up and make a line down almost to the line below the base line. Round it from 4 to 8.

Class repeats the three sounds of o: "ŏ, ō, ōo."
It is a short letter and it starts at 2 on the clock and goes up and way around and closes at 2. Make it sit on the line.

Class repeats the two sounds for s: "s, z."
It is a short letter. It starts at 2 on the clock, goes to number 10, slides across to number 4 and back around to number 8.

Class repeats the sound for qu, "kw." It takes these two letters to say "kw."

They are short letters. The first one starts at 2 on the clock, goes up and around and closes at 2. Without lifting the pencil make a straight line down to the line below and make a flag in the direction in which we write. The second letter sits close. Begin it with a down line, then round from 8 to 4, continue up with a straight line and finish on the base line with a straight down line.

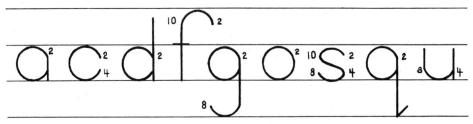

The teacher's explanation of how to use the numbers on the clock is indicated here.

The children's papers should look like this.

Teaching the Letters which Begin with Lines

Teach these line letters as soon as the "clock" letters have been presented well enough to establish in the child's mind the correct ways of forming them.

Letters which start with a line *sit close* to the preceding letter. All beginning lines start at the top. These are two important rules.

Do not take the pencil off the paper to complete any of these letters except in making the second part of k and to put the crosses on f, t and x.

Horizontal lines (including underlining, etc.) are always drawn in the direction of writing, (i.e., from left to right). Never use the words left or right. Instead establish "the direction in which we write", (and read), very firmly at the start. The beginning horizontal lines of e and z and the short crosses on t and f are drawn in the direction in which we write. Make certain that *no* child retraces these lines backwards because this reverses the habit he must acquire.

Class repeats the sound "b."

It is a tall letter which starts with a line. (The lips make a line when saying "b.") Start at the second line above and pull the pencil down to the base line and, without lifting the pencil, go back up almost to the first line above and, going in the direction in which we write, make the round short part starting from 10 and rounding to 8 on the clock.

Class repeats the two sounds for e: "ĕ, ē."

This letter is short. It starts with a straight line drawn from 9 to 3 through the clock. (Put 9 and 3 on the clock face to show this.) Without lifting the pencil continue up around the clock from 3 and stop at 4.

Class repeats the sound "h."

Repeat the directions for b above except that the rounded part goes from 10 to 2 and finishes with a down line to the base line.

Class repeats the two sounds for i: "ĭ, ī."

This is a short letter which starts at the top. The dot is made last.

Class repeats the sound "j."

This is a short letter. Since it begins with a line it starts at the top. It goes down almost to the line below, before rounding on the clock from 4 to 8. The dot is put on last.

Class repeats the sound "k."

The first part is tall and starts at the top. The second part is separate. It is a short part which starts at the top.

Class repeats the sound "l."
It is a tall line which starts at the top and sits on the base line.

Class repeats the sound "m."
It is a short letter that begins with a line. It starts at the top and is drawn straight down to the base line. Retrace to the top and round it on the clock from 10 to 2, continue by making a straight line to the base line, retrace to the top of the line, round again from 10 to 2 on the clock and finish with a straight line which ends at the base line.

Class repeats the sound "n."
This is a short letter. Repeat the directions for making the first part of m above.

Class repeats the sound "p."
It starts with a line and therefore sits close to the preceding letter. The line starts at the top and goes to the line below the base line. Retrace on this line to the top and round the second part from 10 to 8 on the clock.

Class repeats the sound "r."
This is a short letter which starts at the top. Make the short line go to the base line, retrace to the top and round it from 10 to 2 on the clock.

Class repeats the sound "t."
This is a tall letter. It begins at the top. The cross is small and drawn in the direction in which we write.

Class repeats the three sounds for u: "ŭ, ū, ŏŏ."
This is a short letter. It starts with a line at the top. Bring the line almost to the base line and round it from 8 to 4, continue up with a straight line and retrace with a line to the base line.

Class repeats the sound for v.
This is a short letter. It starts with a line and therefore it is started at the top and sits close to the preceding letter. The first line slants in the direction in which we write. Finish without lifting the pencil.

Class repeats the sound of w. The teacher gives the same directions she gave for "v."

Class repeats the sound of x: "ks."
It also is short and the first line starts at the top; therefore it sits close to the last letter and slants in the direction in which we write. The cross is made separately and it starts at the top.

Class repeats the three sounds for y: "y, ĭ, ī."
This is a short letter. Start it at the top with a straight line, then round the bottom from 8 to 4, go up with a straight line and straight down almost to the line below the base line, before rounding from 4 to 8 on the clock. (As a consonant, y has one sound; as a vowel, it has two sounds.)

Class repeats the sound "z."
This is a short letter. It starts with a line. Therefore it sits close to the preceding letter and the top line is made in the direction in which we write. Without taking the pencil off the paper make a slanted line to the base line at the point under the beginning of the top line, and finish with a line drawn in the direction in which we write. The top and bottom lines should be parallel.

The teacher shows how the clock is used on the rounded parts.

The children's papers should look like this.

I have gone into detail as to what to say to children who are learning to write because it is necessary to be specific if handwriting is to become a correct, facile tool for learning. If letters are made incorrectly, they are mentally pictured incorrectly also. This becomes one of the serious causes of failure in both reading and spelling—one of many reasons why correct writing is essential.

Those letters that begin at 2 on the clock have been shown and also those which begin with a line. Now write the alphabet across the page in order to teach the correct spacing of letters. The spacing of letters is taught from the first lesson. Letters that begin at 2 on the clock start just far enough away from the preceding letter to form the clock. Letters that begin with a line sit very close to the preceding letter. Always say the sounds of the letters before writing them. (Note that q alone has no sound.)

The reader may wonder at the amount of detailed directions given to explain the teaching of writing. In these techniques and aids to writing will be found the simple direct system for helping any child acquire the correct motor patterns. Therefore it is worth while to include here every aid that has proven most valuable in teaching, even if the detail seems monotonous to an adult. The first and second grade and kindergarten teachers cannot afford to skip any of it. Handwriting is a basic means of overcoming the confusions and reversals in reading which so many children suffer from.

Techniques of Teaching the Manuscript Capital Letters

Be sure the lower-case letters are well learned before introducing all the capital letters.

It is necessary to teach some of the capital letters early, such as those needed for the first letters in writing a child's name.

When children learn that a capital is used only where the rules of English require it, they will not insert capitals indiscriminately. There is always a definite reason for using a capital letter. Children should be taught these reasons and be required to give the reason each time they use a capital.

All capital letters are tall. They fill the space between the base line and the second line above. (Shown below at half size.)

The rules for round lower case letters also apply to the following capital letters. They each start at 2 on the clock. (Give the sounds of each capital letter before writing it and have the children repeat these sounds before they write.) The cross on the Q starts at the top.

In writing capital letters beginning with lines make the vertical line first, starting at the top. The horizontal lines of A, E, F, H, I, T are made in the direction in which we write. Where there is more than one horizontal line, make the top one first. (E, F, I) The pencil is lifted before making the second lines of A, B, D, E, F, H, I, K, M, N, P, R, T, and they also begin at the top.

ABDEFHIJKL

MNPRTUY

The capital letters V, W and X are made just like their lower-case letters. First make the line which slants in the direction in which we write, starting at the top. V and W are made without lifting the pencil. The second line of X starts at the top.

Y is the only capital which is finished below the base line.

Z is formed the same as its lower-case letter. The top line is drawn in the direction in which we write and it is finished without taking the pencil off the paper.

VWXZ

Techniques of Teaching Numbers

Numbers should be as high as the tall letters. All numbers are the same height.

The numbers 8, 9 and 0 begin at 2 on the clock.

The rule for the spacing of numbers which begin at 2 on the clock is the same as for manuscript letters. Start just far enough away to make a clock.

The numbers 1, 4, 5 and 6 begin with a line and all lines start at the top. The left-hand vertical line of 4 and 5 is drawn first. The horizontal line of the 5 is short and is drawn last and in the direction of writing.

The bottom of a 6 can end on the base line. Then it never looks like 0. 7 begins with a line drawn in the direction of writing.

The numbers which begin with a line sit very close to the preceding number. This is also true for 2 and 3.

Numbers 2 and 3 begin at 10 on the clock. Note that no lower-case letter starts at 10 so these two numbers should be thoroughly understood by children who show confusion in direction.

Now write all the numbers on a line showing the proper spacing. All except the last three which begin at 2 on the clock, start close to the preceding number.

1234567890

Before the children write 2 and 3 ask where these two numbers start until every child knows they begin at 10 on the clock. (Children who reverse these numbers can come to dislike arithmetic. It is very important to prevent this reversing.)

In itemizing or numbering pages, I do not put periods after whole numbers. In mathematics a period is a decimal point and it is read "and." 5.2 is read "five and two-tenths."

In writing the brain directs the hand. This cannot be done correctly unless there is a thorough knowledge of how each letter and number is made.

The child who has no difficulty in learning to write needs to be taught at first, but need not be held for drill. The children who need help should be given the specific directions in this chapter over and over until they can direct their hand in writing and no longer make errors in direction or orientation. This is where drill is an essential part of teaching, if children are to learn. The teacher has done no teaching unless and until the pupil learns.

After the first presentation, it is well to have small groups, in turn, write at the blackboard. Errors in writing can thus be readily caught and corrected.

After teaching the sounds and the writing of single manuscript letters the teacher presents all the other phonograms on the Seventy Cards in varying sequences, but in the same manner as the single letters were presented. The phonograms now should be written in two columns down the page rather than across the page. Have the children fold their papers down the middle and use the crease to line up the second column. The phonograms must be thoroughly learned with the accurate sounds and they must be correctly written (not copied).

Spacing has already been shown so that when a card of more than one letter is written the question "Where does the second or subsequent letter start?" should bring the response, "At 2 on the clock. Start just far enough out to make a clock" or "It begins with a line which sits close to the last letter. A line starts at the top."

When words are introduced the spacing of letters within a word follows the above rules. A space the size of one letter is left between words. (Show the children that on the typewriter, pressing the space bar once leaves such a space.) Children's papers are more easily read if they leave the space of two letters between sentences.

After children can easily form the letters correctly they should learn to reduce the size of their handwriting to one third the size of the above lower case letters. This reduced size is used in showing the cursive writing which follows.

Cursive Writing

Cursive writing follows the same rules for position as those given for manuscript writing.

The letters of connected (i.e., cursive) writing should be taught only after manuscript writing with the phonogram sounds has been perfected by long practice and no longer requires any special attention. This can usually be after Christmas in the second grade. Children want to learn cursive writing. A promise to teach it as soon as they perfect the basic manuscript writing is an incentive to a real effort to improve.

All the letters within a word in cursive alphabet writing are connected together.

The connecting lines from the end of one letter to the right place to start the next letter are of five kinds:

a short upswing from the base line,

a tall upswing from the base line,

a short upswing which curves on over to 2 on the clock,

a short dip kept at the height of a short letter across to the start of the next letter, or as an ending on the letters: b, o, v and w.

the short dip that curves on over to 2 on the clock.

All vertical lines start at the top and are drawn straight down to the base line before starting the sharp curve up.

All letters which go below the base line and curve back up, cross at the underside of the base line at the point where the down line has crossed the base line.

f g j qu y z

The vertical lines in cursive writing can be slanted forward for the right-handed child. All such lines are parallel to each other. Left-handed writers can write straight up and down. If they develop a slant it must be back hand, never forward.

Most of the differences between manuscript and cursive writing are shown by the dotted lines in the cursive letters below. The solid lines show to what extent the letters are alike.

abcdefghijklmnopqrstuvwxyz

abcdefghijklmnopqrstuvwxyz

Cursive writing is easily taught by having the children write the entire manuscript alphabet and then write over it the cursive letters with connecting lines and other changes, as shown above. The differences are readily seen. Be sure all the sounds of each letter are spoken just before it is written.

acdghijlmnopqutuvwxy

b e f k r s z

The forms of a, c, d, g, h, i, j, l, m, n, o, p, qu, t, u, v, w, x, y are essentially the same in cursive writing and in manuscript. The letters b, e, f, k, r, s and z are changed the most, and need more attention.

v and w are written the same as in manuscript except that the lower sharp points are rounded and they end with a dip at the top.

b, e, f, h, k and l start with an upswing which makes a sharp curve backward at the top to start the straight down line.

g, j, y and z are the letters which end with a straight line down below the base line and take a sharp curve backward at the bottom and up to connect to the next letter. This up curve crosses the down line exactly at the base line.

f and q turn forward and swing up, meeting the down line exactly at the base line. The q turns at the bottom as did the flag in the manuscript form.

d and p have no loops.

a, c, d, g, o, and q, letters which in manuscript begin at 2 on the clock, also can begin at 2 in cursive writing when they are the first letters of words.

m, n, u, v, w, x and y may also be made without an initial up line from the base line at the beginning of a word.

---

m, n and x start with a slight curve.

All down lines are straight lines. If they are slanted the slant should be the same for each down line.

All letters at the end of a word or when written alone end with a small upswing from the base line except b, o, v, w, which end with a dip kept at the height of a short letter.

Spacing between words can and should be closer in cursive than in manuscript writing because the end of a word is shown by the absence of a connecting line to the first letter of the next word.

Teachers obtain the attention and effort of their children through their personality and interesting ways of teaching. Teaching requires a little dramatizing to open children's minds for learning. A good teacher intuitively senses whether what she is saying is listened to, is understood, and is likely to be retained. This seems especially true in teaching these language arts.

The Capital Letters in Cursive Writing

Certain capital letters in cursive writing do not connect to the next letter. These are D, F, O, P, V and W.

The capital letters D, E, F, T, G, I, J, L and Q are different forms from the small letters or manuscript letters.

D starts with a straight down line and is completed without lifting the pencil.

E and L begin at 2 on the clock.

I and J are the only letters that begin at the base line with a backward upswing and curve forward at the top. (All upswings for lower-case cursive letters are forward.) I and J should be carefully taught together. As lower-case letters they are the only ones which are dotted. As capitals they are the only ones that begin with a backward upswing.

G and S start alike with an upswing from the base line.

T and F begin with a dip at the top.

Q and Z begin at 10 on the clock as do the numbers 2 and 3.

Other Writing Hints

A comma is a tiny half-clock. It starts on the line comfortably close to the letter it follows, and goes below the line rounding from 12 to 6 on the clock.

When the children first write a period, say, "A period is made by setting the pencil on the line comfortably close to the letter it follows, and taking the pencil up." This keeps children from setting commas and periods just any place, and also gives a precise kinesthetic feel to them. It also helps them to see commas and periods on the printed page.

I am convinced that teachers must demonstrate and explain much more about how each letter, number and punctuation mark should be formed and placed. The strange, awkward ways in which nearly all children contrive to form some of their letters shows their need of all these techniques of handwriting.

The first letter written on a page should be written carefully because every letter that follows should be of the same relative size.

Every round letter should fit on the same-sized clock.

Tall letters and capitals are twice as high as short letters.

All letters which go below the base line go just as far below the base line as short letters go above it.

I have given a great deal of study to the techniques of teaching good and easy handwriting, not only for its own sake but also for the facility for self-expression and for clarifying of one's ideas that come from a command of easy, readable writing. The prime reason is that it is the simplest direct means of learning the sounds of English as they are represented in our written language. I do not know of another book on handwriting which at every point ties in the sounds of the letters with their form. And yet what meaning can the form of a letter have unless it conveys its sound to the child as he learns to write it? This is one of the reasons why writing is the logical road to reading.

CHAPTER V

The Child's Notebook

THIS CHAPTER demonstrates in detail the method by which each child above the second grade writes the first seven pages in his own notebook every year. It is his own reference book for the phonograms and for the rules of spelling and pronunciation. (The teachers in the first two grades put appropriate parts of these pages on the blackboard and then on charts for ready reference in teaching the rules of spelling as they are needed.)

Spelling rules, explanatory notes and instructions for the teacher are given along with each page of the model of the child's first seven pages of his notebook.

The teachers in the first and second grades, as well as those in the upper grades, need to be fully conversant with this entire notebook and its explanations in order to teach and explain correctly any word that comes up in speech, writing or reading.

It should be noted here that pages 1, 2, 5, 6 and 7 of the notebook are basic. Their contents are taught from the start in all grades even though the children in the first two grades do not write this part in a notebook.

I want to emphasize that the teacher or parent who gives careful attention to the procedure and meticulously follows all the major and

94

minor details of teaching for the mental and physical production of this notebook, will be well rewarded. Progress of each and all of her pupils will henceforth make her work much lighter and a source of pleasure. The mastery of the notebook is the key to the child's success in his use of the language arts. This is where competent teaching really counts.

In presenting the writing of the notebook to the children of the third grade and each higher grade, the teacher should tell what the purpose of the notebook is. (I have taught many classes of high-school students and many young people of college age who have needed and have written this notebook.) It is presented in manuscript unless the students already know cursive writing.

I teach manuscript writing at first to each student no matter what his age. The older student needs manuscript for lettering maps, diagrams and drawings, but chiefly it makes a needed visible link between his writing and all printed matter. All children should first write the phonograms given on the cards in manuscript. This gives them a kinesthetic connection between the sounds and printed forms for reading. For those with any reading handicap this is highly important.

Detailed Technique for Teaching Page One

The first page lists the single consonants at the top. It gives the single vowels and words to show the important sounds of each vowel. At the bottom of the page are listed the five kinds of silent final e's.

The teacher tells the children that the first word "Consonants" is the title or name for the next line of letters. The word Consonants goes in the middle of the top line. Since it is a title, we write it with a capital. We divide it into syllables.

A syllable is that part of a word or a single word which is capable of being pronounced by a single impulse of the voice. Once when teaching a group of ninth-grade boys who had no idea what a syllable was I used my hands to indicate the beat of the syllables. Take the word consonants. After the class says, "con" the teacher, facing the class, makes a down beat with her right hand. The class says "so" and her left hand makes a down beat. For "nants" she crosses the right over the left for the final beat. The children, in showing syllables in this manner, start with the left hand, then the right and then the left crossed over the right hand. This kinesthetic effect has proven helpful to many children and can even be used with pre-school children to establish correct pronunciation.

To go a step further in the kinesthetic feel of a word the teacher holds up three fingers of her right hand showing that it takes three letters to write the first syllable and points to the finger on her right. The children say the sound "c"; as she points to the next finger they say "ŏ"; and as she points to the next one they say the sound "n." Then the teacher holds up two fingers of her left hand. She points to the one to her right and the children say the sound "s." She then points to the other finger and the children say "ō" showing there are two letters to write so. Then crossing the right hand over the left she holds up five fingers for nants and points to each in turn as the children give the individual sounds.

These procedures give children who have difficulty learning to spell a chance to think what the writing must be, before they actually write. Such reasoning keeps children from making errors which once made must be supplanted later. This is good teaching.

The teacher asks the children to give her the first syllable of Consonants. When she gets the reply "Con," she writes it on the board. At the same time the children are writing it in their notebooks. (They write while she is writing because they are not to copy her writing.) While writing Con, the teacher asks for the second syllable. When she gets the reply "so," she puts it on the board while the children write it in their books. While writing so, the teacher asks for the third syllable. When she gets the reply "nants," they write nants while she writes it, and they sound out "n," "ă," "n," "t," "s." This helps them to write it accurately. This sounding of the phonograms should always be done with any syllable which presents a difficulty in accurate pronunciation or in writing.

The teacher then says, "On the next line we will write the single consonants." (These are printed in order on the first 21 phonogram cards.) She asks, "The first consonant in the alphabet says what?" as she holds up the card b. The children give the sound "b" (not "bŭ") and write the letter. She then shows the card c and the children say "k", "s" for the two sounds of c and write the letter c. (Since no consonant ever uses its name for its sound, we never say the names of these letters when it is possible to use their sounds instead.)

The children should know the phonograms and give the sounds in unison. Before they write, they are reminded of how each letter is made in case any child is not sure of it. Continue writing the rest of the consonants in the same manner.

On the third and fourth lines write, "c before e, i or y says $\overset{2}{c}$. If g is before e, i or y it may say $\overset{2}{g}$." The teacher has the children say and write each of the phonograms in these words as they are written. She will have previously studied the Ayres list (which follows in Chapter VI) and will know how to teach these words just as described in Chapter VI. The above description of writing the word "Consonants" is identical with this, except that in one-syllable words each phonogram is sounded before it is written.

The teacher tells what is to be written and where. Everything which is written must also serve as continued training in the accurate writing of the sounds and sequences of speech.

On the next line the children write the title "Vowels" using exactly the same procedure as described for the title "Consonants." Here we put a 2 above the s. In this case and where figures above phonograms may be written hereafter, the figure above a phonogram indicates that the word uses the phonogram's second sound or the third, etc. These sounds are always numbered in the sequence as listed on the backs of the phonogram cards. When no figure is written above, it signifies that the first sound is the one used in the word. (Numbers are not needed above the phonograms c and g because simple rules tell which sound to use.)

The single vowels are on the phonogram cards 20, and 22 to 27.

The five kinds of silent final e have a special way of being numbered. On all seven pages of the notebook and also in the Ayres list in Chapter VI, all these silent final e's are identified by the numbers 2, 3, 4 or 5 written below them. If the e belongs to the first kind of silent e, no number is put under it.

The other pages of the Child's Notebook are presented in the same manner as described above.

Notes to Teachers about Page One

This page presents the twenty-one single-letter consonants, the six single-letter vowels, and the five kinds of silent final e's.

This is a spelling notebook. In it words when written alone are divided into syllables so that the relationship between the sounds and the symbols can be readily seen.

Each consonant has but a single sound except c, g and s. The Rules 2 and 3 below make it unnecessary to number the second sounds of c and g. Only s when it says "z" needs a 2 placed above it when learning to pronounce and write words.

I avoid using the terms "name" of a letter, "the long vowel" or "short vowel." Instead I use the sound itself because the other words are only names for sounds and are thus less direct.

The children must learn and understand and always apply the following seven rules.

Rule 1. q is always written with two letters qu when we say the sound "kw." The u is not considered a vowel here.

Rule 2. When c by itself has a sound, it always says "s" if followed by e, i or y (cent, city, cyclone); otherwise its sound is "k" (cat, cyclone, music).

A model of Page One of the
Child's Notebook.

Con so nants

b c d f g h j k l m n p qu r s t v w x y z

c before e, i or y says ĉ, and

if g is before e, i or y it may say ĝ

Vow elṡ

a	at	na vy	wȧnt³
e	end	me	
i	{In di an	si lent	
y	{ba by	my	
o	odd	o pen	do³
u	up	mu ŝic²	pu̇t³

Silent final e {
tim e
hav e =2
chanc e =3
lit tle =4
are =5

blue =2
charge =3

(no job e)

In many words ci is pronounced "sh", and then it is a two-letter phonogram and thus does not have either sound of c. ch is always a two-letter phonogram. Rule 2 applies only where c is a single phonogram.

Rule 3. When g has a sound by itself it can say "j" only if it is followed by e, i or y. When followed by any other letter, it says "g." (Get, girl and give prove that there are a few exceptions to this rule.) In spelling if g is used to say "j," it must be followed by e, i or y, as in pigeon, religious.

These rules 2 and 3 are most valuable. They enable the child to know the correct sound for c and g by means of the letter that follows. The teacher should ask for these rules until the children apply them automatically, in both writing and reading.

The vowels are underlined in key words only when they say their name at the end of a syllable. The child learns the sounds of the vowels in the order given. The first one is used most frequently. A child may need to say the key word to prove that his sound is accurate until he is sure of each sound. For example if he does not say the ŭ in just correctly he can help himself by saying the first sound of the key word, up and then sounding "j" "ŭ" "s" "t."

Rule 4. Vowels a, e, o, u usually say "ā," "ē," "ō," "ū" at the end of a syllable. The second key word shows this: (na vy, me, o pen, mu sic.) This is one of the three ways a vowel may say ā, ē, ī, ō or ū.

Rule 5. i and y can say "ī" at the end of the syllable but usually they say "ĭ." This is shown at the end of the second syllable of both Indĭan and babў.

Rule 6. y, not i, is used at the end of an English word.

Rule 7. There are five kinds of silent e. In short words, as me, she, he, the e says "ē" but in all longer words where a single e appears at the end, the e is silent. (There are very few exceptions.) In Chaucer's day they were sounded. Now they are silent. As shown below we retain the first four kinds of silent e's because we need them. The fifth kind is probably a relic from Chaucerian days.

1) time. This is an "ī," then a consonant, and a final e. The silent e is put there to make the i say "ī" instead of ĭ. This is true in late, here, style, rose, tune. The single vowels before any single consonant can say "ā," "ē," "ī," "ō" or "ū" if a silent e follows to end the base word. (Sometimes there are two consonants between as in paste or bathe. These words are past and bath when the silent e is omitted.)

2) have, blue. In English we cannot end a word with v or the single vowel u. We add a silent e. (Impromptu is one of the few exceptions.)

3) chance, charge. The silent e follows c and g to make them say "s" and "j." Without the e, the last sounds would be "k" and "g." Rules 2 and 3 show this. At the end of a base word we could use only e as a silent letter. (i cannot sit at the end of a word and y always has a sound at the end of a word.)

4) lit tle. Every syllable in English must contain at least one vowel. ble, cle, dle, fle, gle, kle, ple, sle, tle and zle are the only syllables where neither of the first two letters is a vowel and the silent e is added in each so they can be separate syllables.

5) are. The e is not needed for any of the above reasons. It has no job and we call it the "no job e." House, come, promise are other examples of silent e's which perform no useful purpose in present-day English.

All of the above facts about our language can be learned from page one. The teacher should make constant reference to this page and to the six pages that follow to illustrate facts about our language as the children learn to write and read. This gives them understanding and security in speaking, writing and reading.

A model of Page Two of the
Child's Notebook.

Her	first	nurse
fern	third	hurt
herd	bird	burn
din ner	girl	church
berth	birth	turn
west ern	fir	fur
merge	thirst	pur pose
perch	firm	hur dle
gro cer y	squirm	sur prise
serv ice	squirt	Thurs day
verse	chirp	Sat ur day
nerve	cir cle	fur ther
nerv ous	sir	oc cur
ster ling	con firm	fur nish
per fect	skirt	dis turb
clerk		sub urb
cer tain		cur tain

works	early.
worm	learn
word	heard
world	search
worth	earn
wor thy	ear nest
worse,	pearl
worst	earth
wor ry	re hears al
wor ship	

Notes to the Teacher about Page Two

Her first nurse works early.

This sentence gives five spellings of the sound "er" and it should be memorized. Their phonogram cards are numbered 27 to 32. The spelling er is used most often.

Rule 8. or may say "er" when w comes before the or, as in works. There are few other guides in the choice of the spelling of the sound "er."

First dictate the sentence containing the five spellings of the sound "er." It sits on the top line of this page. Teach each word as described for teaching words on page one. Then dictate the five words across the second line, and so on.

Check the children's knowledge of this page by asking, for example, "Which "er" is in church?" The answer is, "The one in nurse." (The word in the model sentence at the top of the page.) Do this same checking with any word having an "er" sound.

For children who find spelling difficult it is advisable to consider or and ar as having only the sounds as in for and far—not the sound er as in doctor and collar. In speaking, the or of doctor and the ar of collar deteriorate in sound because the accent is on the first syllable. In writing them say "doc tor" and "col lar."

Notes to the Teacher about Page Three

First dictate the four headings of the columns, then the top word of each of the first three columns, then the three words on the line below and so on for the three columns. Then dictate the exceptions from top to bottom. Children readily learn the nonsensical sentence given and learn that all these words plus the few at the bottom of the column contain ei. From the headings on this page it can be seen that there are three places for the use of the phonogram ei. The cards 56 and 57 show the three sounds each for ie and ei and two of these are the same for both phonograms. Therefore the sound alone cannot show which of these spellings to use. Rule 9 helps to decide which phonogram to use.

Rule 9. After c we use ei. If we say "ā" we can use ei, but never ie. In the list of exceptions we use ei. In all other words we use ie.

---

ie is "ĕ" in fri̲e̲nd. Put two lines under it. These double lines are used to mark any such phonogram which has an uncommon sound that is not given on the phonogram cards.

eigh is not considered on this page because this phonogram should say "ā." It is not ei alone. In foreign the ei has a sound, and the gn has a sound. They are not one sound as is eigh.

The teacher will test each child by asking which spelling, ie or ei, is used in the listed words. Example: Which is used in receive? In answering the child should say, ei because it comes after c; or, if the word is brief, he will say "ie because it comes after r and not after c, also the sound is not "ā," and it is not one of the exceptions."

I find that if children, in this way, apply and state these rules often enough they will begin to apply them when they write. It is the old problem of teaching children to think before they write or speak. It helps them develop the vital habit of using their minds in what they do and say.

I have asked many children in classes and individually how they know when to use ie or ei. Almost all know the rhyme ī before ē except after c, or when sounded as ā, etc. Then I have asked, "Which do you use after c?" It was a year and a half after I began asking this in the six upper grades in several schools before any child was able to give me the answer. So you see a rule that is not understood and used is of small value.

A model of Page Three of the
Child's Notebook.

We use ei after c, ___ ___ ___ ___

ie	cei
be lieve,	re ceive,
be lief	per ceive,
fierce,	ceil ing
brief	re ceipt
niece,	con ceit
priest	
field	
siege,	
friend	
chief	
a chieve,	
piece,	
pie	
lie	
prai rie	

_ _ _ _ if the sound is "ā," _ _ _ _ _ _ _ and in some exceptions.

ei says "ā"	Exceptions	
their (they)	Nei ther	
veil	for eign	
skein	sov er eign	Learn
heir (in her it)	seized	this
rein	(the) coun ter feit	as a
reign	(and) for feit ed	sentence
vein	lei sure.	
sur veil lance		
	ei ther	
	weird	
	heif er	

Notes for the Teacher about Page Four

This page explains the usual spellings for the sound "sh" at the beginning of any syllable after the first one. Cards No. 67, 68 and 69 show these.

Dictate these words, after the column headings and a general discussion of Rules 10 through 13, by going from top to bottom of each column in turn. (Be sure the words are dictated as said in conversation, but that the children say each separate syllable just before they write it.)

Rule 10. sh is used at the beginning of a base word and at the end of a syllable (she, finish) but, except in the ending ship (friendship, worship,) it is not used at the beginning of any syllable after the first.

Rule 11. ti, si and ci are the phonograms most frequently used to say "sh" at the beginning of a second or subsequent syllable.

Rule 12. si is used to say "sh" when the syllable before it ends in s (ses s̲ion) and when the base word has an s at the point where the base word i̲s changed (tense, ten s̲ion).

Rule 13. s̲i saying "zh" is on this page to remind us that si is the only common phonogram for the "zh" sound (di vi s̲ion).

---

ci is used in gracious and facial because the base words, grace and face, have c where the change comes.

In some words no rule governs the choice of ti, si, or ci for the sound "sh" and the spelling must be memorized, as in influential.

It is important that the vowel sound in each of the last syllables of the words on this page be said accurately.

Vĕ ne t̲ian (ă), im pa t̲ient (ĕ), gra c̲io̲us (ŭ)

The first s of conscious and conscientious is silent. The ci of associate and the first ci of conscientious say "sh" but since there is no vowel except the i of ci in these syllables, the i is sounded. The syllable ci says "shĭ."

Is the cie in the word ancient an exception to Rule 9 illustrated on page 3 in the notebook? No, because this is ci followed by an e which fact we know from their sounds in this syllable. Unless the phono-grams are sounded aloud many rules of spelling do not make sense. It is the failure to combine the sounds with the spelling of English which makes it seem so difficult to learn and makes so many common words seem to be exceptions to the general rules of spelling. This is another good reason why it is important always to teach any new word by writing its spoken sounds.

The use of the sounds of the phonograms permits the child to see clearly the relationship between the spoken word, the writing of the word and the reading of it.

After every lesson in the making and using of the notebook, each listed word written should be read aloud by the child, first in syllables and then again as the word is said in conversation. He should also use the word in a sentence which shows that he knows its meaning.

A model of Page Four of the
Child's Notebook.

sh is used at the beginning of a base word,
at the end of a syllable but not at the beginr
of any syllable after the first one. ti, si and ci

ti	si
na tion	ses sion
im par tial	com pres sion
sub stan tial	dis cus sion
pa la tial	de pres sion
po ten tial	ad mis sion
pa tience$_3$	
tor ren tial	ten sion (tense)$_5$
in fec tious$_4$	tran sient (trans sit)
in flu en tial	man sion (manse)$_5$
am bi tion	
su per sti tious$_4$	
con fi den tial	s^{2}i
col lec tion	
Ve ne tian	di vi s^{2}ion
	oc ca s^{2}ion
	ex plo s^{2}ion

usually used to say "sh" at the beginning of a syllable after the first one.

	ci	
ån cient		
ra cial		
so cial		
fi nan cial		
{gla cial		
{gla cier		
e lec tri cian		ce
fa cial		
gra cious		o cean
phy si cian		
mu si cian		
pro fi cien cy		
con scious		
as so ci ate		
con sci en tious		

Notes to the Teacher about Page Five

This page shows when final consonants are doubled when certain endings are added to base words.

Rule 14. Words of one syllable (like hop), ending in one consonant, which have only one vowel before this last consonant, double the last consonant before adding an ending that begins with a vowel.

The order of dictating the words on Page 5 is important. The base words on the left-hand page are dictated first. Then dictate the endings which begin with a vowel and discuss how we add the appropriate endings to the base words. (Reasoning is required to use Rules 14, 15 and 16).

Now dictate the second column on the left-hand page. The children should understand that they are using Rule 14 as they write. A quite different intellectual process is required in writing the double consonant in base words, such as the two l's of village or trolley.

The child must learn that he doubles the p in "hopping" to preserve the vowel sound of the base word hop (ŏ). If the p is not doubled the word is hopĕd whose base word is hope as shown on Page 6.

Writ is the archaic past tense of write. We still use "writ" as a noun. Explaining this can help to show why we say "writ ten."

Check to see that the child understands Rule 14. Ask, "How do you add the ending ment to ship?" The child's answer should be, "We do not double the p of ship because ment is not one of the endings which requires it. ment begins with a consonant, not a vowel."

Ask, "How do we add "ĕd" to talk?" The child should reply, "We do not double the k since this base word ends in two consonants, not just one."

Ask, "How do we add "er" to red?" The child replies, "We double the "d" since red has one syllable, one consonant at the end, one vowel before the last consonant and the ending begins with a vowel. Rule 14 can be called the one, one, one rule.

Rule 15. Words of two syllables, like "begin," where the second syllable gin is like hop, having one consonant at the end and one vowel before it, also double this last consonant before adding an ending that begins with a vowel, if the accent is on the last syllable.

Americans use this rule more consistently than do the English.

Ask the children to clap the rhythm of two-syllable words where the above rule applies as they pronounce them. (Notice that acquit conforms to the rule since the qu is a consonant sound. The u is not considered a vowel here.)

Words that have the accent on the first syllable, but otherwise would fit the rule, should be clapped also. We should not double the consonant in these words when adding an ending beginning with a vowel:

en′ ter, prof′ it, can′ cel, trav′ el

A model of Page Five of the
Child's Notebook.

Words of one syllable, ending in one consona[n]
which have only one vowel before this last co[n]
sonant (like hop), double the last consonant [be]
fore adding an ending that begins with a vow[el]

hop	hop ping hopped[3]
run	run ning
stop	stopped[3] stop page
red	red dish
hot	hot test
mud	mud dy
flat	flat ten
drug	drug gist
ship	shipped[3] ship per
writ	writ ten

	ing ice[3] ous[4]
	er ish ist
Endings which	[3]ed age i ble[4]
begin with a {	est {ance[3] {a ble[4]
vowel	y {ant {a bly
	al {ence[3] {an cy
	en {ent {en cy

Words of two syllables, (like begin, where the second syllable gin is like hop, having one consonant at the end and one vowel before it), also double this last consonant before adding an ending which begins with a vowel, if the accent is on the last syllable.

be gin′	be gin ning
ad mit′	ad mit tance
ac quit′	ac quit tal
oc cur′	oc cur rence
ex cel′	ex cel lent
trans mit′	trans mit ter
for got′	for got ten
con trol′	con trol la ble
re mit′	re mit ted

Notes to the Teacher about Page Six

Rule 16. Words ending with one of the five kinds of silent e's drop the e when adding an ending that begins with a vowel. (hope— hoping)

The child must be well taught to see that these endings are appended to a base word, and to recognize what that base word is.

Sometimes we cannot drop the e. Changeable holds the e to let the g say "j," since able begins with a vowel, but not an e, i, or y which would permit g to say "j." (See Rule 3) Such exceptions can be easily understood by children who know the basic rules about c and g.

The e of hope is dropped for the past tense ending "$\overset{3}{e}$d." In hop$\overset{3}{e}$d the e has two functions. It permits the o to say "ō" as well as forming "$\overset{3}{e}$d" as an ending.

The dictionary says to drop the final e of fierce to add the ending est, but in speaking, to put the c on the last syllable. This allows us (under Rule 2) to keep the "s" sound of c instead of its k sound.

Rules 14, 15 and 16 should be taught and well understood as they are needed even in the first grade. Pages 5 and 6 along with Pages 1 and 2 of the Notebook are basic for all grades.

A parent or teacher who is under the impression that six-year-olds lack the mental ability to learn, understand and apply such rules will be surprised and delighted to see how quickly they all do so, and how keen they are about demonstrating this ability to use reasoning in their work.

Words like hope which end with a silent e, drop the e when an ending beginning with a vowel is added.

A model of Page Six of the Child's Notebook.

hope	hoped hop ing
de sire	de sired de sir ing
nerve	nerv ous
be have	be hav ior
fierce	fierc er fierc est
ease	eas y
come	com ing
change	chang ing
serve	serv ice
re hearse	re hears al
set tle	set tling set tler
write	writ ing

Endings beginning with a vowel

ing	ice	ous
er	ish	ist
ed	age	i ble
est	ance	a ble
y	ant	a bly
al	ence	an cy
en	ent	en cy

A model of Page Seven of the
Child's Notebook.

Additional Common Phonograms. The number
preceding a phonogram tells how many sounds it
has.

sh	3) oo
ee	
2) th	3) ch
{ ay ai	ng
	3) ea
2 { ow 4 { ou	ar
	ck
{ oy oi	3) ed
{ aw au	or
	wh
2 { ew 2 { ui	oa

3) ey	$\left\{\begin{array}{l} ti \\ \text{2) } si \\ ci \end{array}\right.$
3) ei	
3) ie	
igh	
eigh	
$\left\{\begin{array}{l} kn \\ gn \end{array}\right.$	6) ough
wr	
ph	
	$\left\{\begin{array}{l} eu \\ pn \\ rh \\ \overset{2}{qu} \\ \overset{2}{x} \end{array}\right.$
dge For	
Grade VI	
oe and above	
gh	

Notes to the Teacher about Page Seven

The single consonants are listed on page one of the Child's Notebook and words containing these sounds are on the phonogram cards. The single vowels (with words to prove their sounds) are also on page one of the Child's Notebook.

Page two of the Child's Notebook gives five spellings of the sound "er" and a sentence showing all five, which the children learned, (Her first nurse works early.)

The phonograms on this page are all those not given on the first and second pages. They are numbered 32 through 70 on the phonogram cards. All the 70 phonograms are now in the Notebook and thus readily available at all times for both teacher and children.

The following examples of the sounds of these phonograms in words are for the teacher. The words should not be taught to the child because he should not associate these phonograms with any special word. He is to know them, and their sounds, when he writes or sees them in any word.

sh	(di<u>sh</u>)
ee	(s<u>ee</u>)
th	(<u>th</u>in, <u>th</u>is)²

ay	(d<u>ay</u>) used at the end of a syllable.
ai	(p<u>ai</u>nt) Used in the middle of a word, never at the end.

ow	(n<u>ow</u>, l<u>ow</u>² "ō")
ou	(r<u>ou</u>nd "ow," f<u>ou</u>r² "ō," y<u>ou</u>³ "ōō," c<u>ou</u>n try⁴ "ŭ")

oy	(b<u>oy</u>) Used at the end of a syllable.
oi	(p<u>oi</u>nt) Used in the middle of a syllable.

aw	(l<u>aw</u>)
au	(f<u>au</u>lt)

ew   (grew "$\bar{oo}$," new "$\bar{u}$")

ui   (fruit "$\bar{oo}$," suit "$\bar{u}$")

oo   (boot "$\bar{oo}$," foot "$\bar{oo}$," floor "$\bar{o}$")

ch   (much, school "k," chiv al ry "sh")

ng   (rang)

ea   (east "$\bar{e}$," head "$\breve{e}$," break "$\bar{a}$")

ar   (far)

ck   (neck "k") Used only after a single vowel when it does not say its name.

ed   (grad ed, loved "d," wrecked "t")

or   (or)

wh   (when)

oa   (boat "$\bar{o}$")

ey   (they "$\bar{a}$," key "$\bar{e}$," val ley "$\bar{i}$")

ei   (con ceit "$\bar{e}$," veil "$\bar{a}$," for feit "$\bar{i}$")

ie   (field "$\bar{e}$," pie "$\bar{i}$," lil ies "$\bar{i}$")

igh   (sigh "$\bar{i}$"

eigh   (weigh "$\bar{a}$")

kn   (knot "n") Used only at the beginning of a base word.

gn   (gnat "n")

wr   (write "r")

ph   (phan tom "f")

dge   (bri<u>dge</u> "j") May be used only after a single vowel which
              does not say its name.

oe   (t<u>oe</u> "ō")

gh   (<u>gh</u>ost "g")

⎡ **ti**   (na <u>ti</u>on "sh") (See page 4 in the Child's Notebook.)
⎢ **si**   (ses <u>si</u>on "sh," vi <u>si</u>on "zh")
⎣ **ci**   (fa <u>ci</u>al "sh")

                ⎡ th<u>ough</u> "ō"
                ⎢ thr<u>ough</u> "o͞o"
ough   ⎢ r<u>ough</u>   "ŭf"
                ⎢ c<u>ough</u>   "ŏf"
                ⎢ th<u>ough</u>t "aw"
                ⎣ b<u>ough</u>   "ow"

   The following phonograms are not listed on the 70 phonogram
cards. They are to be taught in Grade VI and above. They may be
introduced separately at an earlier time if they are needed.

eu   (<u>Eu</u> r<u>ope</u> "ū")

pn   (<u>pn</u><u>eu</u> m<u>o</u> ni ā "n") kn, gn, pn are alike in sound.

rh   (<u>rh</u>i noc <u>er</u> os "r")

q̇u   (mos q̇<u>u</u>i t<u>o</u> "k")

ẋ   (ẋ<u>y</u> l<u>o</u> <u>ph</u><u>one</u> "z")

Spelling Rules

For convenient reference the rules given in the Teacher's Notes about the first seven pages of the Child's Notebook are listed below in the same order. Additional useful spelling rules are appended and numbered for reference.

Almost no rule is absolute. It is well to make this clear and to say that we shall all be on the lookout for words that do not conform to the rules. Such words can be readily learned and a little drill is needed for them. In the whole Ayres list of a thousand words which are given in Chapter Six less than fifty have any part which does not agree with the sounds on the phonogram cards or with these rules of spelling. However all these rules hold true often enough to be very helpful. It makes a good and useful game to have the children "discover" words where the rules do not apply. That way they make an impression not quickly forgotten. Finding soccer where we drop the sound of the second c, or facade where c says "s" and is not followed by e, i or y, are examples.

Rule 1. q is always written with 2 letters, qu, when we say "kw." The u is not considered a vowel here. (See Page 1 of the Notebook.)

Rule 2. When c by itself has a sound, (not part of a two-letter phonogram) it always says "s" if followed by e, i or y (cent, city, cyclone). If not followed by one of these letters its sound is "k," (cat, claw, cyclone). This is true in spelling and in reading. (See Page 1 of the Notebook.)

Rule 3. When g has a sound by itself it can say "j" only when followed by e, i or y. When followed by any other letter it says "g." (Get, girl and give prove that there are a few exceptions to this rule.) In spelling, if you use g to say "j" it must be followed by e, i or y—as in pigeon, religious. (See Page 1 of the Notebook.)

Rule 4. Vowels a, e, o, u usually say "ā," "ē," "ō," "ū," at the end of a syllable. This is one of but three ways a vowel may say ā, ē, ī, ō or ū. (See Page 1 of the Notebook.)

Rule 5. i and y can say "ī" at the end of a syllable but usually they say "ĭ." This is shown at the end of the second syllable of both Indĭan and babў.

Rule 6. y, not i, is used at the end of an English word. (Taxi is short for taxicab and macaroni is an Italian word. Words like these should be explained when they are met.) (See Page 1 of the Notebook.)

Rule 7. There are five kinds of silent e. (See Page 1 of the Child's Notebook.) These five silent e's are indicated by special markings in this book, as shown at the bottom of Page 1. The notes to teachers for this page explain these five kinds of silent e's.

Rule 8. or may say "er" when w comes before the or, as in work. (See Page 2 of Notebook.)

Rule 9. After c we use ei.

If we say "ā" we can use ei, but never ie. In the list of exceptions we use ei. In all other words using ie or ei we use ie. (See Page 3 of Notebook.)

Rule 10. sh is used at the beginning of a word and at the end of a syllable (she, finish) but except in the ending ship (friendship) not at the beginning of any syllable after the first one. (See Page 4 of Notebook.)

Rule 11. ti, si, ci are the spellings most frequently used to say "sh" at the beginning of a second or subsequent syllable. (See Page 4 of Notebook.)

Rule 12. si is used to say "sh" when the syllable before it ends in an s (ses sion), and when the base word has an s where the base word changes (tense, ten sion). (See Page 4 of Notebook.)

Rule 13. si (not ti or ci) can also say "zh," as in division.

Rule 14. Words of one syllable (like hop) ending in one consonant, which have only one vowel before this last consonant, always double the last consonant before adding an ending that begins with a vowel. (See Page 5 of Notebook.)

Rule 15. Words of two syllables, like begin, where the second syllable gin is like hop, having one consonant at the end and one vowel before it, also double this last consonant before adding an ending that begins with a vowel, if the accent is on the second syllable. (See Page 5 of Notebook.)

Rule 16. Words ending with one of the five kinds of silent e's drop the e when adding an ending that begins with a vowel. (When the ending does not begin with an e, i or y the silent e is retained so that g can say "j" as in changeable, or so the c can say "s" in noticeable.) (See Page 6 of Notebook.)

Rule 17. In English we often double l, f, s following a single vowel at the end of a word of one syllable, as in will, off, glass, roll. Children must learn where these come and then they must learn words like recess, distaff, egg and add, when they meet them.

Rule 18. ay is used to say "ā" at the end of a word, rather than a alone, except for the article a.

Rule 19. A vowel may say its name if it is followed by two consonants (find, old).

Rule 20. s never follows x. There is an s sound in x (ks).

Rule 21. All, written alone, has double l, but written with another syllable only one l is used: al so, al most.

Rule 22. When till and full are added to another syllable we drop one l: un til, beau ti ful.

Rule 23. dge may be used only after a single vowel which does not say its name, as in bridge.

Rule 24. When adding an ending to a word that ends with a y that has a sound alone, change the y to i unless the ending is ing: carry is changed to carried and carries but in carrying we keep the y. In English we almost never have an i follow i. In the words played, boys, we do not change the y since it is ay and oy, and not y alone for its sound.

Rule 25. ck may be used only after a single vowel when it does not say its name, and only at the end of a syllable, or at the end of a base word.

Rule 26. Words which are the individual names or titles of people, of places, of books, of days and months, etc., are capitalized. (Mary. Honolulu, Amazon River, Bible, Monday, July)

CHAPTER VI

The Application of the Phonograms and the Rules

THIS CHAPTER gives children the needed training in the use of what they have been learning about writing the sounds, and about the rules of spelling. A thousand words most commonly used in English are taken from the "Ayres List" from *Measuring Scale for Ability in Spelling* by Leonard P. Ayres.* The words are dictated by the teacher, in the order given. The child says only the first phonogram of a one-syllable word and writes it. As he writes that sound he says the next one, and so on until he finishes the word. For words of more than one syllable, he says the first syllable and starts to write it. Before he finishes writing it, he says the next syllable, writes it and so on. This eliminates saying the whole word before starting to write. He does not say the names of the letters unless the sound and the name are the same. He should say only the sound of the phonogram. This permits the child to write about as fast as he can speak distinctly.

The dictionary has been followed as closely as possible for sounds for teaching spelling. I use but three sounds each for a, o and u, and two sounds each for e, i and y. This promotes far more accurate speaking than usually can be found in our schools.

In pronouncing each syllable before he writes it the child should

---

* Educational Testing Service, Princeton, N. J.

stress the vowel wherever possible in order to be in agreement with the spelling. In normal speaking or reading, the rhythm of speech and sentence accent, as well as word accent, reduces very naturally many of such stressed vowels to their dictionary pronunciation. The dictionary states that a monosyllable word (or a syllable of a longer word) when pronounced alone, always stresses the vowel. This conforms to the spelling but sometimes differs slightly from the proper pronunciation when it is spoken in context. This stressing of vowel sounds makes spelling much more phonetic and easy to learn. WEBSTER'S COLLEGIATE DICTIONARY, the 1953 edition, explains on page ix the correct variations in pronouncing words in different contexts and uses.

The teacher dictates the whole word as spoken in normal conversation (not by syllables) to the children. She then gives a sentence containing the word. The teacher's sentences can restate useful facts such as how the children should sit or hold their pencil, form letters, facts about how the language works, etc. She can tell the children how good they are at reasoning, studying, playing, and even insert philosophical ideas about learning. They need not be dull, unimaginative sentences, but they should be short, and models of English. They serve as a standard for the type of sentences she wants from the children when their turn comes to use the word in a sentence.

Whenever a spelling rule accounts for the spelling of a word, it is explained with that word. These rules are not so much to be memorized as they are to be taught as facts about the language which the teacher helps the children to discover. In this way the children sense the meaning of each rule instead of having a mere parroted memorizing of it, a most important difference.

The following five items explain the simple markings of the words of the Ayres list which are used to impress on the children how the rules and phonograms actually work.

1) A vowel is underlined at the end of a syllable when it says its name.

m̠e

o̠ pen

Ju̠ ly̠

(Spelling Rule 5 states that i and y usually say "ī" at the end of a syllable. Where this is true i and y are not underlined— fam i ly.)

2) <u>Phonograms of two or more letters are underlined.</u>

    <u>th</u>in

    bri<u>dge</u>

    <u>eigh</u>t

3) <u>Silent letters and phonograms when their sound is one not given on the phonogram cards, have a double line under them.</u>

    ha͇lf (We say "haf" but write half.)

    fri͇end (ĕ is not one of the sounds on card 57 for ie.)

The silent e at the end of a base word is one of five different kinds and each kind is marked as shown below. All except the first kind have a number below to show which kind it is. (See the teacher's notes for page 1 of the Notebook.)

    ti͞me

    have͇₂   blue͇₂

    chance͇₃   charge͇₃

    lit tle͇₄

    are͇₅

4) <u>Numbers are placed above a phonogram when its sound is not the first sound given on its card.</u> (Except where a line is used under a vowel which says its name at the end of a syllable.)

    dŏ³   lo̲w²

    wăs³²   yo̲u³

    pŭt³   co̲un try⁴

           tho͇ught⁵

           bo͇ugh⁶

5) <u>Some words are bracketed together.</u> In such cases the first word is in the Ayres list. The others have been added to show (1) the base word, or (2) several words with the same peculiarity in spelling, or (3) how some words are said alike but use different phonograms in spelling, or (4) contrast in the sounds of two words that might easily be confused.

Techniques of Presenting the Words of the Ayres List.

These words are to be presented orally by the teacher. The children do not see these words until they write them from dictation.

The teacher says the first word "me" and gives a sentence containing me. The word is not unfamiliar. The meaning is clear and the only problem is how to write it.

The children give the first sound "m." As they start the writing of "m" they say "ē" and write e. They underline the e and the teacher points out that under Rule 1 a, e, o, u say their names at the end of a syllable. The children then read me aloud.

The teacher then dictates "do" and gives a sentence containing do. The children say "d" and before finishing the writing of "d" they say "ōo," write o, and put a 3 above it. In the initial presentation the teacher says, "We write the letter which says 'ŏ, ō, ōo.'" They then read "do."

All of these words are to be taught just as described above and in the notes to the teacher regarding the first seven pages of the Child's Notebook. First- and second-grade children will not have written in notebooks these seven pages but will be taught the rules and facts which these seven pages contain as these points come up in the words of the Ayres list. They will however have their own notebooks in which to write the words dictated from the Ayres list. The third and upper grade children first write the seven pages of the Child's Notebook, (which they should correct until they have an exact model just as shown in Chapter V), and they follow this with the dictated words.

After each word is written a child should read it and give a sentence containing the word. This latter may well be postponed until all the words in the day's lesson are written.

Almost all of this list of 1000 words are in the spoken or "understood" vocabulary of normal six-year-old children. Teachers should of course introduce and teach no words far beyond the easy understanding of the children in their age group. It seems silly to mention this but critics of phonics seem to assume that if the sounds of the language are taught the meaning of individual words and sentences is overlooked. Experience with our phonics is quite the reverse and such criticism quite unfounded.

Words in Sections A to H (From the Ayres List)

(Study the above techniques and the five numbered explanations of underline and number markings.)

me   **Rule 4.** (e says "ē" at the end of a syllable)

do³   The third sound on the phonogram card for o is "ōō"

and

go   **Rule 4.** (o says "ō" at the end of a syllable)

at

on

a   **Rule 4.** (a may say "ā" because it ends the syllable. In speech when the accent is not on a its sound becomes "à" as shown in the dictionary. For spelling say "ā.")

it

is²   (s says "z," the second sound on its card)

she̲   Rule 4. (It takes two letters to write the sound "sh.")

can

se̲e̲   (We use the two letter card ee to write "ē" in see. When
        children are writing words for the first time the teacher
        tells them which phonogram the dictionary uses where
        there are several possibilities.)
run

²
the̲   Rule 4.

in

so̲   Rule 4.

no̲   Rule 4.

now̲   (There are two cards for the sound "ow." We use ow
        here since English words should not end with u.)

man

ten

bed

top

he̲   Rule 4.

³
yo̲u̲   (The third sound on the card for ou is "ōō." You and
        thou are two of the few words that end with ou. y at
        the beginning of a word is always the consonant y. This

is important for reading only, since in translating sound there is but one phonogram given for the consonant "y.")

will   **Rule 17.** (We often double l, f, s, following a single vowel at the end of one-syllable words.)

we   **Rule 4.**

an

my   **Rules 5 and 6.** (English words do not end with i. We use y which has the sounds of i.)

up

last   (We use s, not c, since Rule 2 shows c would say "k" here.)

not

us

am

good   (The second sound for oo is "o͝o.")

lit tle   (Page 1 in the Notebook gives the five silent final e's. tl sound but the e is silent. Child says "lit" and writes it, then "tle" and writes it. In the spelling lesson words should be written in syllables. In writing sentences, of course, they cannot be divided.)

Using the two hands to give the kinesthetic feel of the two syllables helps here.

a̲ go̲   **Rule 4.** (Child says "ā" and writes it, then "go" and writes it. In reading or speaking ago, the accent is on go and therefore the full sound "ā" cannot be said. This deterioration in sound is caused by the rhythm of English speech which must always be taught in reading and in speech.)

o̊ld   **Rule 19.** (A vowel may say its name if followed by two consonants.)

bad

red

of̲̲   (We say "v" but write "f." Both must be learned. Put two lines under f. They indicate here that the sound we write for spelling is different from the sound in speech.)

be̲   **Rule 4.**

but

²this̲

²
åll   The teacher tells that we use the letter that says "ă, ā, ah" when the children give the first sound of all.

Rule 17. (The third sound of a is "ah" on its phonogram card. This is a slight overtone used here for spelling.)

³
yo̲ur   (you is the base word of your)

³
yo̲u

out   In the first presentation the teacher shows the ou card (which says "ow, ō, ōō, ŭ") to write the first sound of out.

time   No. 1 on page 1 of the Child's Notebook. "ī," consonant, e. We put the silent e on so the i can say "ī." Without the e the word would be Tim.

The child has now met the three usual ways for a vowel to say its name: 1) by ending the syllable (me),

    2) by having two consonants follow it (óld), and

    3) by being followed by a consonant and a silent e (time).

It follows that the o of of should say ŏ, the u of but should say ŭ, etc.

may   **Rule 18.** (At the end of a word we use ay to say "ā" rather than a alone, except in the article a.)

in tó

him

tó day   **Rule 18.**

look   The teacher tells that we use the card that says "ōō, ŏŏ, ō" to say "ōō" in look.

    Rule 25. (We could not use ck at the end.)

did

like   Page 1 of the Notebook. We need the silent e so the i can say "ī."

    (We must use k, not c, to say "k.")

lice

six

boy	**Rule 6** shows why we would not use oi here.
book	**Rule 25.**
by	**Rule 6.**
have	Refer to the five kinds of silent e on page 1 of the Child's Notebook. The a says "ă" but we still need the e. English words do not end with v.
are	Page 1 of the Notebook. This is a silent e with no job.
had	
o ver	**Rule 4.** (Page 2 of the Child's Notebook gives the spellings for "er." This er we use most often.)
must	
make	Page 1 of the Notebook. The e makes the a say "ā." We could not use c to say "k" because we need the e so the a can say "ā" and the e would make a c say "s."
school	(The second sound of ch is "k.") It takes four phonograms to write school.
street	It takes five phonograms to write street.
say	**Rule 18.**
come	Page 1 of the Notebook. This silent e has no job.
hand	
ring	Be sure each child says ng correctly.

live   The e makes the i say "ī."

live₂   Page 1 of the Notebook. The i does not say "ī" in live₂ but we need the silent e since no English word may end in v.

kill   **Rule 17.** (We use c at the beginning of common words when we can. Here we cannot for it would say "s.")

late   The e makes the a say "ā."

let

big

moth er   (Page 2 of the Notebook gives the spellings of the sound "er." We use er more often than the other four. The dictionary says we say "ŭ" instead of "ŏ." The overtone "ŏ" can be said in saying individual syllables for spelling. The rhythm when saying the syllables together causes the lower sound "ŭ."

three

land

cold   **Rule 19.**

hot

hat

child   **Rule 19.**

ice   The e makes the i say "ī."
         Rule 2 is secondary here.

pl<u>ay</u>   **Rule 18.**

⌈ s<u>ea</u>   ee and ea (each saying "ē") show that the words have dif-
⌊ s<u>ee</u>   ferent meanings.

Section H

Do not relax nor shorten the method of presenting the following words. Follow in detail the same procedure in teaching each word
as outlined at the beginning of the Ayres list.

d<u>ay</u>   **Rule 18.**

<u>ea</u>t   The teacher tells that the dictionary gives the ea card ("ē,
                ĕ, ā") for the ē sound in eat. The child should soon be
                able to give this information to the teacher when eat is
                dictated in subsequent lessons. Drill is necessary on such
                words.
sit

lot

box   (x = "ks" in sound)

be lo<u>ng</u>   **Rule 4.**

⌈ do͞͞or   (door and floor are the only words in *The Ayres list* in
                which oo says "ō." In all other words oo will say "o͞o" or
⌊ flo͞or   "o͝o."

yes

lo͞w

soft

stand

y<u>ar</u>d

bri<u>ng</u>

tell   **Rule 17.**

f<u>i</u>v<u>e</u>   (The e makes the i say "ī." This is its primary job.)

b³all   **Rule 17** (The third sound for a is "ah" as shown on its phonogram card and on page 1 of the Note-book. This is a slight overtone here for spell-ing.)

l<u>aw</u>   (We use aw, not au, at the end of a word since u should not end a word.)

ask   (k, not ck, is used because a consonant sits before. ck can be used only after a single vowel which does not say its name.)

just   (We must write j here, for g would say "g" since it is not
gust   followed by e, i or y.)

w<u>ay</u>   **Rule 18.**

get

h<u>o</u>m<u>e</u>   The e makes the o say "ō."

mu<u>ch</u>

cȃll   Rule 17.

lo<u>ng</u>

lo<u>ve</u>₂   The e is needed since no English word may end in v.

<u>then</u>

h<u>ouse</u>₌₅   The ou sound in house is from the card ou (which says "ow, ō, ōō, ŭ"). The e has no job.

y<u>ea</u>r   (Year takes three phonogram cards.)

tȯ

<u>I</u>   (We always write a capital I because this word stands for one's own name: Mary, John, etc. This is one of the few exceptions to Rule 6.)

aš

send

one   (Spell one by saying the names of the letters if necessary. We probably once said one as in lone and ȯnly which mean one. Phonetically we would say "on." Since we say "won" (the dictionary deteriorates the sound to "wun"), the correct spelling must be learned. of and one are the only words in the first grade list where sound and

haš   written form are not the same.)

som<u>e</u>₌₅   The e has no job.

if

how

her

them

oth er

ba by   (y says "ī." Be sure the children say "ī." To write babies
we change the y of baby to i and add es.)

well   Rule 17.

a bout

men

man

for

ran

run

was   (The first time was is sounded and written the teacher
tells phonograms to use. The next time the children will
tell which phonograms we write.)

that

his

led

lay   **Rule 18.**

(This is the point of minimum accomplishment for a first grade.)

end 1st grade

Section I

The five kinds of silent e found on Page 1 of the Notebook will no longer have a notation after them. They will be underlined and numbered as they are on Page 1 of the Notebook.

nine

face   (c can be used since we put an e after it. The children must learn to write c in this word. Drill is necessary.)

miss   **Rule 17.**

ride

tree

sick   **Rule 25.** (ck is used here after a single vowel.)

got

north

white   (wh has no sound but air can be felt on the hand held before the lips. Ask children to blow air out and feel it on their hands. "white" not wite.)

spent

foot

blōw
²

block

spring

riv er   (The child says "riv" and writes it, if he can, without
sounding the individual sounds. Before finishing the
writing of riv he says er and writes that.)

plant

cut

song

sing

sang

sung

win ter

stone

free

lake

lace

page

nice

end

fȧll   Rule 17.

f<u>ee</u>t

went

ba<u>ck</u>   Rule 25.

<u>a</u> wa<u>y</u>

p<u>a</u> per

pŭt   We use the u card (which says "ŭ, ū, o͝o.")

<u>ea</u>ch

s<u>oo</u>n

c<u>a</u>m<u>e</u>

Sun da<u>y</u> Rule 26. (Sunday is the day's own name and ·like a child's own name, John White, must be written with a capital letter. Sunday was named for the sun.)

shoẇ<u>w</u>

Mon da<u>y</u> Rule 26. (Monday is the day's own name and must be written with a capital letter. Monday was named for the moon.)

m<u>oo</u>n

yet

find   Rule 19.

give₂

new   ew says "ū."

let ter

take

Mr. = Mister   In Mr. we left out 4 letters and put a period at the
end. When we leave out letters of a single word and
put a period at the end we call this an abbreviation.
Rule 26. Mr. is always written with a man's name
(Mr. Brown).

af ter

thing

what·   Be sure children do not say "watt" for "what."

than

its   (Its is used as we use hers or his.)

it's = It is   The apostrophe is used in place of the i of is. When we
put words together and leave out some letters, we put in
an apostrophe where letters are omitted. This is a contraction.

ver y   The e says "ĕ." Three phonograms are needed to write
ver. y says "ĭ."

o̲r̲

tha̲nk   (We say "thangk" but for spelling say "th," "ă̱," "n," "k.")

de̱a̱r

west

so̊ld   Rule 19.

to̊ld   Rule 19.

best

fo̱rm

fa̱r

ga̱ve̲

a̱ like̲

add   (Learn to double the d. Addition needs both d's.)

Section J

sev en

fo̱r get

hap py   (y says "ĭ.")

no̲o̲n

think

sis ter

cast

card

south

deep

in side

blue

post   Rule 19.

town

stay

grand

out side

dark

band

game

boat

rest

e<u>a</u>st

⌈ son   Sound ŏ for spelling.

⌞ sun

help

h<u>ar</u>d

r<u>ace</u>

cov <u>er</u>

⌈ f<u>ire</u>   (Be sure the children say "r" and do not say "fi er.")
              These words have but one syllable.

  w<u>ire</u>

⌞ t<u>ire</u>

<u>age</u>

gō²ld   Rule 19.

⌈ r<u>ea</u>d   (a book)

⌊ rĕ²<u>a</u>d   (a book)

⌞ red

f<u>ine</u>

can not

May   Rule 26.

may

line

left

ship

train

saw

pay

large₃

near

down

why   (Not "wy")

bill

w³ant

girl   (Page 2 in Child's Notebook.)

part

still

place

re port

nev er

found

side

kind   Rule 19.

life

here

car

word   Rule 8. (Page 2 of the Notebook.)

ev er y   Rule 5.

un der

most   Rule 19.

made

said   (Say ā when writing. Its base word is say. We say "sed"
              in speaking. Both the writing and the reading must be
              learned since the two are different.)

say

work   Rule 8. (Page 2 of the Notebook.)

our

more

when

from

form

wind

wind   (the clock) **Rule 19.**

print

air

fill   Rule 17.

a long

lost

name

room

hope

same

glad

with

mine

At this point we should discuss base words and derivatives. Many words are derived from "base" words and it is always important for word meaning, grammar and a grasp of how the language is formed that the base word be taught with each derived word. For example, please is the base word for pleasant, pleasure, displease, etc. It is important also that the children learn that, although many words contain the spellings of shorter words which are not related in meaning —this fact is a mere coincidence which they should ignore. The phonics teaching now being used in many schools classifies rhyming words like ill, will, bill, fill, kill, mill, etc., as word families. This is wrong. They are not families but completely unrelated words.

Section K

be came

broth er

rain

keep

start

mail

male

fe male

eye

I

(eye is not phonetic. The picture gives the spelling and the meaning of eye. This is the only word in *The Ayres list* where a picture is helpful in learning the spelling of a word.

glass

par ty   y says "ĭ."

up on

twȯ   (For spelling say the sounds of the three letters we write. Two is not phonetic. We probably once said "two" sounding the "w" as we still do in twin and twain.)

twin

twain

they

would   (Sound as it is written for spelling. We say wọod.)

an y   (Sound "ă" as it is written for spelling. We say "ĕ" in normal speech and in reading.)

man y

could   (Sound the 4 sounds as they are written for spelling. We say cọod.)

should   (Sound the 4 sounds as they are written for spelling. We say shọod.)

cit y

on ly (The base word is one.)

where₅ (Not wear)

⎡ week

⎣ weak

first (Page 2 in the Notebook.)

⎡ sent

⎣ cent

mile

⎡ seem (Base word is see.)

⎣ see

e ven

with out

af ter noon

Fri day **Rule 26.** (Friday was named for Frigga, the wife of Odin, in Norse Myth.)

⎡ hour (For spelling pronounce the h as it is written. Compare meaning with our.)

⎣ our

wife

state

Ju ly   Rule 26.

head

sto ry

o pen

short

la dy   (y says "ī.")

reach

bet ter

wa ter

round

cost

price

be come

class   Rule 17.

horse

care

try

move₂

de lay   Rule 18.

pound

be hind   Rule 19.

a round

burn   (Page 2 of the Notebook.)

camp

⎡ bear

⎣ bare

clear

clean

spell

poor

fin ish

hurt   (Page 2 of the Notebook.)

ma̲y be̲   (It may be—is the meaning.)

a̒ cross   Rule 17.

to̊³ night   (We use three letters to say "ī.")

ten̲th̲

sir̲   (Page 2 of the Notebook.)

these̲²

those̲²

club

seen   (Base word is see.)

see

felt

fů³ll   Rule 17.

fa̲il̲

set

stamp

li̲ght

com ing̲   (Page 6 of the Notebook.)

come̲₅

cent   (Compare meaning with sent.)

sent

night

pass   Rule 17.

shut

ea$\overset{2}{s}$ y   (Page 6 of the Notebook.)

ea$\overset{2}{s}$e₅

Section L

catch   (Pronounce the "t" in writing)

black   Rule 25.

warm

un less   Rule 17.

$\overset{2}{cloth}$ ing   (Page 6 of the Notebook.)

$\overset{2}{clothe}$

be gan

be gin

be gun

a̱ ble̱₄

⌈ gone̱₅

go̱

done̱₅   (Say ŏ for writing.)

⌊ do̊³

su̲i̲t²   (ui says "ū.")

track̲   Rule 25.

wå³tch̲   (Pronounce t, in writing.)

das̲h

fell   Rule 17.

fig̲ht

⌈ bu̱y̲   (Sound "ŭ" in writing. Discuss meaning.)

⌊ by̲

stop

⌈ wå³l̲k̲   (Sound as written for spelling. We say "wȧ³k," "tȧ³k,"
            "bȧ³k.")

│ tå³l̲k̲

⌊ bå³l̲k̲

grant

s**oa**p   This oa may be taught as the "ō" in the key word boat.

n**ew**s

n**ew**

sm**a**ll   Rule 17.

w**ar**

sum m**er**

a bo**ve**

ex press   Rule 20.

t**ur**n   (Page 2 of the Notebook.)

les son

ha**lf**   (Sound 1, for spelling. We say "haf.")

f**a** **ther**

an y **thing**   (Say ă in writing.)

t**a** b**le**

hi**gh**

t**a**lk   (Sound 1 in writing.)

June   Rule 26.

right

write

wrote

date

road

rode

ride

March   Rule 26.

march

next

in deed

four

her self

pow er

wish

be cause

w**or**ld   (Page 2 of the Notebook.)

c**oun** try

⎡ m**ee**t

⎣ m**ea**t

an o**th** er

trip

list

pe **o** pl**e**   (Children enjoy saying 3 syllables for writing. We say
              "pe ple")

ev **er**

held

church   (Page 2 of the Notebook.)

⎡ on**ce**   (Base word is one. Neither one nor once is phonetic. We
⎢   say "won**ce**" and "won.")
⎣ one

own

be f**ore**

⎡ kn**o**w

⎣ n**o**

were

where   (These four words have the same last three letters but they are not all said alike. Each is phonetic, however.)

there

here

dead

leave

ear ly   (Page 2 in the Notebook.)

close

close

flow er

flour   (The last sound is "r," not er.)

noth ing

ground

lead   (the way)

led   (the way)

lead   (pencil)

such

m<u>a</u>n y   (Say "ă," when writing. We say "men y.")

m<u>o</u>rn i<u>ng</u>

h<u>ow</u> ev <u>er</u>

m²ind   Rule 19.

<u>sh</u>all   Rule 17.

<u>a</u> l<u>one</u>

<u>or</u> d<u>er</u>

<u>th</u>ir<u>d</u>   (Page 2 of the Notebook.)

p³u<u>sh</u>

p<u>oi</u>nt

wi²<u>th</u> in

done

do

gone

go

bod y   (y says "ĭ.")

(This is the point of minimum accomplishment for a second grade.)

Note to teachers. For spelling ask the children to say polysyllable words in syllables. When the word is written, ask them to read it in syllables and then read it again as a word in proper English rhythm.

By now Rules 4, 5, 6, 7, 8, 17, 18, 19, 25 should be understood. They will no longer be noted.

Section M

trust

ex trä̇

dress

be side

teach

hap pen

be gun

col lect   (We often have the 2 sounds "c" and "t" at the end of a word: direct, elect, protect. Sound each carefully.)

file

pro vide

sight

stood

fix

b**or**n

góes̲   (Learn: Add e̲s̲ to go, do and Tu to make goes, does
               and Tuesday.)

g**o**

do**es̲**

do̊

T**ue̲**s day̲

ho̊ld

drill

ar my

pre̲t ty   (Say ĕ for writing only. We say "prit ty.")

st**o̲le̲**

in com**e̲**₅

boůght

p**ai̲**d   pa**y̲**   (The base words are pay, lay and say. We change the
                 form of these words and do not add ed to the base
l**ai̲**d   la**y̲**   words.)

s**ai̲**d   sa**y̲**   (We write "s**ai̲**d" but we say "sed." Both must be
                 learned.)

en ter

rail road (The rails are on the road.)

un a ble

tick et

ac count We cannot say ā here. When the sound is definitely ă the
vowel is followed by a consonant. (ăr rive, ăf fect, ăp pear)

driv en

re al

re cov er

moun tain   (Sound it as it is written for spelling. We say "moun
ten.")

steam er

speak

past

might

be gin

con tract

deal

al mŏst   Rule 21.

all

broūght

less

e vent

off

of

true₂

tŏŏk

a gain   (Sound it as it is written for spelling. We say "a gen."
          The British say it as it is written.)

in form

bŏth

heart   (Not phonetic. We say "hart" but write heart. The doc-
          tor listens to your heart with his ear.)

month

chil dren

child

bu¹ ild   (We say "bild.")

bu¹ ilt

un de̲r stand

fol lo̲w²

charge₃

says²   (Sound it as it is written for spelling. We say "se²s.")

say

mem be̲r

case

while   (Not "wile.")

³al so   Rule 21.

re turn   (Page 2 in Notebook.)

²tho²se

²the²se

of fi̲ce₃

gre³at

Miss

miss

who   (Sound it as written for spelling. We say "hŏ.")

died   (The e serves two functions: ie says "ī" and ed says "d.")

die   (Page 3 in the Notebook.)

change   (The e makes the a say "ā" even though there are two
          consonants between. The e also permits the g to say "j"
          but this is a secondary job.)

wire

few   (ew says "ū.")

please

pic ture

mon ey   (ey says "ĭ.")

read y

o mit

an y way   (Sound as it is written for spelling.)

an y

way

Section N

ex cept   (c followed by e, i or y may follow x. See Rule 20.)

aunt   (Sound as written for spelling.)

ant

cap ture

wrote

write

else

bridge   Rule 23.

of fer

suf fer

bu ilt

bu ild

cen ter

front

rule   (Say ū for spelling.)

car ry

chain

death

learn   (Page 2 in the Notebook.)

won der

tire

pair   (two)

pear   (eat)

pare   (cut)

check

prove

heard   (Page 2 in the Notebook.)

hear

in spect

it self

al ways   Rule 21.

some thing

write

wrote

ex pect   Rule 20.

nee̲d

²
thus

⎡ wo̲ man   (Sound as written for spelling. Came from wife man.

⎣ wo men   Then say "woom an" and "wim en.")

⁴
you̲ng

⎡ fai̲r

⎣ fare

dol la̲r

⎡ eve ni̲ng

⎣ eve

plan

bro̲ke

fee̲l

⎡ sure   (s here says "sh" in normal speech. Sound "s" for writ-
             ing.)
⎢   ³
⎣ sug ar

le<u>a</u>st

s<u>o</u>r ry

press

God   Rule 26.

god

t<u>each</u> <u>er</u>

N<u>o</u> vem b<u>er</u>   Rule 26. This is the ninth month of the old Roman year. (novem or nine)

sub ject

<u>A</u> pril   Rule 26.

his t<u>o</u> ry

c<u>au</u>s̱e₅

stud y

him self

mat <u>ter</u>

u<u>s</u>e

th<u>ough</u>t

p<u>er</u> son

n**or**   (Explain the use of nor and or.)

or

Jan u a ry   Rule 26. (We say "Jan u ĕr y." Named for Roman god, Janus.)

mean

vote

co²urt

cop y

act

been   (Sound as it is written for spelling. We say "bin." The British say "been." Base word is be.)

be

yes ter day

a mong

ques tion   (Sound as it is written for spelling. We say "ch" here for ti.)

quest

doc tor

hear

si̲ze̲ Few words use z. Size, dozen, organize, citizen are about the only ones in the first 1000 words.)

De̲ cem be̲r **Rule 26.** (This was the tenth month of the Roman calendar. Decem means ten)

doz en

the̲re̲ Rule 26.

tax

num be̲r

Oc to̲ be̲r **Rule 26.** (The eighth month of the Roman calendar. Octo means eight.)

rea s̲on

fif̲th̲

Section O

eight

ate

a̲ fra̲i̲d

un cle̲

ra̲th̲ er

com fo̲rt

e lect

a board   (This is the "ō" we use in boat. The use of the word
            boat should come to distinguish this spelling of "ō"
            from the several others.)

jail

shed

re tire

re fuse

dis trict

re strain

roy al

ob jec tion   (Page 4 of the Notebook.)

ob ject

pleas ure   (Comes from please.)

meas ure

treas ure

na vy

fourth

four

pop u la tion   (Page 4 of the Notebook.)

prop er

judge   **Rule 23.**

wéath er   The first sounds of these two words are different.

wheth er

worth   (Page 2 of the Notebook.)

con tain

fig ure

sud den

for ty   (Why the our is changed to or in forty is not obvious.
         The spelling must be learned.)

four

fourth

four teen

in stead

throw

threw

per son al

ev er y thing

rate

chief   Rule 9. (Page 3 of the Notebook.)

per fect

sec ond

slide

far ther

du ty

in tend

com pan y

quite

quit

qui et

knew

know

re main

di rect

ap pear

lib er ty

e nough

fact

board   (We use the ō of boat.)

Sep tem ber

sta tion   (Page 4 of the Notebook.)

at tend

be tween

pub lic   (We seldom use c at the end of a word.)

mu sic

pic nic   When adding ing we use ck to keep the "k" sound. (pic-nick ing)

friend   (ie says "ĕ") Page 3 of the Notebook

dur ing

en dure

through

po lice   (The children will enjoy saying this as it is written for spelling. We say "po lece.")

un til   **Rule 22.**

mad am

tru ly   (Learn to drop the e of true when writing truly. The e is used at the end of true because we do not end words with true   a single u. In truly it is no longer needed, and it is dropped even though the ending does not begin with a vowel.)

whole   (Sound as it is written for spelling.)

hole

ad dress

re quest

raise

Au gust

Tues day (Learn—Add es to Tu, go and do.)

goes

does

struck

get $\underline{\underset{=}{t}}$ing   (Page 5 in the Notebook.)

get

dŏn't = dŏ not   (The apostrophe shows where a letter has been left out. Don't is a contraction. We contracted two words into one word.)

Thur$\overset{2}{\underline{s}}$ d$\underline{ay}$ (Page 2 in the Notebook) (Thursday is Thor's day.)

Sat $\underline{ur}$ d$\underline{ay}$ (Saturday is Saturn's day.)

Ninety-five per cent of these words are strictly phonetic.

(This is the point of minimum accomplishment for a third grade.)

Section P

spend

en j$\underline{oy}$

$\underline{aw}$ fŭl   Rule 22.

$\underline{awe}$

u $\overset{2}{\underline{su}}$ al

com pl$\underline{ai}$nt

$\underline{au}$ t$\underline{o}$

v$\underline{a}$ c$\underline{a}$ $\underline{t}$ion

bea u ti fŭl³   (Sound as it is written for spelling. We say "bu
ti ful.")

bea u ty   *2 syllable*

flight

trav el

rap id   (This word is said as its meaning indicates. There is not
time for a double p sound.)

re pair

trŏu ble₄

dŏu ble₄

en trance₃

im por tance₃

im por tant

car ried   Rule 24. (The ie says "ī" and ed says "d." The e has two
functions.)

car ry   (y says "ĭ.")

loss

for tune

em pire

may or

wait

beg

de gree

pris on

en gine

vis it

guest   (The gu go together as do qu. The u has no sound. In
        this case if the g were next to the e it could say "j.")

guess

de part ment

ob tain

fam i ly

an i mal

fa vor

Mrs. = Mis tress   (The period means that some letters of the
                   word are not written. Mrs. is an abbreviation
                   for which we say "Mis is" in speaking.)

Mr. = Mis ter   (Here we chose the first and last letters for the
                   abbreviation.)

Miss   (Needs no period since the whole word is
                   written.)

hus band (A husband gives his wife a band ring.)

a mount

hu man

vi ew   (The dictionary gives "vū." Sound the ĭ for spelling.)

e lec tion   (The t of elect went over to form ti.)

e lect

clerk

though

o'clock   (Means "of the clock." f and the are left out in this contraction of three words to a word of two syllables.)

sup port

does   (Add es to do and go to make does and goes.)

goes

re gard

es cape

since

which   (Not witch)

length (Sound ng correctly.)

long

strength

strong

de stroy

news pa per

daugh ter (Few words use augh, so this phonogram was not put
on a card. Learn.)

naugh ty

caught

taught

an swer (Sound the w when writing until the spelling is learned.)

re ply

o blige (We would not use dge here since we say "ī.")

sail

sale

cit ies Rule 24. (Change the y of city to i and add es. The ie
says "ī.")

cit y

known

know

sev er al

de sire

near ly

Section Q

some times

de clare

en gage

fi nal

ter ri ble

sur prise (Page 2 in the Notebook.)

pe ri od

ad di tion

em ploy

prop er ty

se lect

⎡ con nec <u>tion</u>

⎣ con nect

f<u>i</u>rm   (Page 2 in the Notebook.)

⎡ r<u>e</u> <u>g</u>ion   (gi says "j." Without the i the last syllable would say
           "gon."

⎣ r<u>e</u> li <u>g</u>ion

con vict

pr<u>i</u> vat<u>e</u>₅   (The ă deteriorates to "ĭ" in normal speech according
            to the dictionary.)

com mand

d<u>e</u> b<u>ate</u>

cr<u>ow</u>d

fac t<u>o</u> ry

pub li<u>sh</u> Rule 10.

rep r<u>e</u> ²sent

t<u>er</u>m   (Page 2 in the Notebook.)

sec <u>tion</u>

⎡ rel <u>a</u> tiv<u>e</u>₂

⎣ r<u>e</u> l<u>ate</u>

prog ress

pro gress

en tire

pres i dent

pre side

meas ure

fa mous   (ous means full of; famous means full of fame.)

fame

serve₂   (Page 2 in the Notebook.)

es tate

re mem ber

ei ther   (Page 3 in the Notebook.)

ef fort

im por tant

im por tance₃

due₂

dew

in cl**u̲d̲e**

run **n̲i̲ng**　　(Page 5 in the Notebook. The double n in running
run　　　　　　is not the same as the two l's in allow. The double n
　　　　　　　in running is a reasoned one which the child must
　　　　　　　remember to do.)

al l**o̲w**

p**o̲** s̲i̲ t**i̲on**

f**i̲e̲ld**　　(Page 3 in the Notebook.)

le**d̲ge**　　Rule 23.

cl**a̲i̲m**

pr**i̲** m**a̲** ry

re s̲ult

Sat **u̲r** d**a̲y̲**　(Page 2 in the Notebook.)

ap p**o̲i̲nt**

in f**o̲r** m**a̲** t**i̲on**

wh**o̲m** *objections*　(Sound as written for spelling. We say "hŏm.")
　　　　recall

wh**o̲** *does*

ȧr rest

them selves   (Learn: Change "f" of self to "v" and add es.)

self

calves   (Sound the 1 for spelling.)

calf

halves   (Sound the 1 for spelling.

half

spe cial   (e says "ĕ" here. Page 4 in the Notebook.)

es pe cial ly

wo men   (Sound as written for spelling.)

wo man

pres ent

pre sent

ac tion

act

jus tice

just

gen tle man

gen tle

en clo͟se͟ (with 2 over close)

a wa͟i͟t

sup po͟se͟ (with 2 over pose)

won de͟r fu͟l (3 over u)   Rule 22.

di rec t͟ion

for wa͟rd

back wa͟rd

to͟ wa͟rd *(oa over to)* 1 syllable   (Sound as written for spelling, and then say "to͟ erd" for speech.)

al t͟hough (3, 2 over al though)   Rule 21.

prompt   (Sound p and t carefully.)

at tempt

who͟se͟ (3 2 over, 5 under) *possessive* (Sound as written and then say "ho͟s͟." (3 2))

who͟ (3 over)

sta͟te͟ ment

sta͟te͟

pe͟r haps

the͟i͟r (2 2 over)   (Page 3 in the Notebook.)

the͟y͟ (2 over)

im pris² on

> writ ten   (Page 5 in the Notebook. Think of the archaic form
>   writ as the base word.)
>
> writ

ar¹ range   (The first a says "ă." The second a has 2 separate con-
             sonants between it and the silent e.)

(This is the point of minimum accomplishment for a fourth grade.)

Section R

> fore noon   (before noon)
>
> be fore

> lŏse₅³²
>
> loose₅   *Tooth*   (Learn: "loose tooth." Both words use oo to say "ōo.")
>
> loss

> com bin a tion
>
> com bine

av en ue₂

neigh bor

weigh

wear³

en ter tain

sal a ry

vis² i tor

vis² it

pub li ca tion

ma chine   (Sound as written for spelling. Then read "mă shēn.")

en gine₅

to ward   (Sound as written for spelling. Then read "to erd.")

suc cess

drown

a dopt

se cure

hon or   (Sound the h for spelling.)

prom ise₅

wreck

pre pare

ves sel

bus̲̈ y [2]   (Sound as written for spelling and then read "bis̈ y.")

bus̲ i ness - 3 syllable

⎡ pre̲ fer̲
⎢
⎣ pref er̲ ence̲̲ [3] (This does not follow Rule 15. The accent changes.)

⎡ il lus tra̲te̲
⎢
⎣ il lus tra̲ tion̲

⎡ dif fer̲ ent
⎢
⎣ dif fer̲

ob ject

pro̲ vi si̲on [2] Rule 13.

ac cor̲d ing̲

al [3] re̲ad [2] y   Rule 21.

at ten tion̲

ed u̲ ca̲ tion̲

⎡ di rec tor̲
⎢
⎣ di rect

pur̲ pose̲̲ [5]   (Page 2 in the Notebook.)

com mon

di a mond

to geth er

con ven tion

in crease₅

man ner

fea ture

ar ti cle₄

> serv ice₃   (Page 6 in the Notebook.)
>
> serve₂

> in jure
>
> in ju ry

ef fect

dis trib ute

gen er al

to mor row

con sid er

a gainst   (Sound as written for spelling. Then read "ȧ genst.")

a gain   (Sound as written for spelling. Then read "ȧ gen.")

gain

com plete

search   (Page 2 in the Notebook.)

treas ure

pop u lar

Christ mas   (The Mass of Christ. Sound t for spelling.)

Christ   Rules 19 and 26.

in ter est

Section S

of ten   (Sound t for spelling. Then say "of en.")

stopped   (Page 5 in the Notebook.)

stop

mo tion

the a ter   (Be sure to accent the 1st syllable in speech: the' a ter.)

im prove ment

im prove

⌐ cen tu̲ ry

└ cent

to̲ tal

men t̲ion

ar ri̲v̲e̲ [1]

sup pl̲y

as sist

dif fe̲r ence̲ ₃

⌐ ex am in a̲ t̲ion   (Sound as written for spelling. We say "eg zam
               in a tion.")
└ ex am ine̲ ₅

pa̲r tic u̲ la̲r

af fa̲ir

⌐ co̲urse̲ ₅ *direction orderly study*

└ co̲arse̲ ₅ *not fine*

nei̲ t̲he̲r [2]   (Page 3 in the Notebook.)

lo̲ cal

⌐ ma̲r ri age̲ [1]   (Sound in 3 syllables for spelling. Then say "măr ige̲ ₃.")
               2 syllables
└ ma̲r ry [1]

căr ri age (Sound as written for spelling. Then say "căr ige.")

căr ry

fur ther (Page 2 in the Notebook.)

se ri ous

doubt (Sound b for spelling.)

con di tion

gov ern ment

gov ern

o pin ion (In these 7 words i uses the consonant sound of y. Since i and y are sounded alike as vowels, i with a

on ion consonant sound of y is not too surprising.)

un ion

fa mil iar

be hav ior (Page 6 in the Notebook.)

com pan ion

mil lion

be lieve .(Page 3 in the Notebook.)

sys tem

pos si ble

pos si bly

piece₃   (Page 3 in the Notebook.)

peace₃

cer tain   (Page 2 in the Notebook.)

wit ness

in ves ti gate

there fore

be fore

too   Means: 1) also; 2) more than enough.

two

to *- relation*

pleas ant

please₅

Section T

guess   (gu are together for the sound "g.")

guest

cir cu lar   (Page 2 in the Notebook.)

cir cle₄

ar gu ment   (Learn to drop the e of argue. We need the e in argue,
only because a u should not end a word.)

ar gue $_2$

vol ume

or gan ize

sum mon

of fi cial   (Page 4 in the Notebook.)

of fi cer

of fice $_3$

vic tim

es ti mate

ac ci dent

in vi ta tion

in vite

ac cept

im pos si ble $_4$

con cern

as so̲ c̲i a̲te̲   (Page 4 in the Notebook. ci says "sh," and since it
                  has no other vowel as in official, the i is sounded. ci
                  here says "sh̆i.")

au̲ to̲ mo̲ bile̲₅

⌈ vär² i o̲u̲s⁴

⌊ vär² y

  ver¹ y

⌈ de̲ ci̲d̲e̲

⌊ de̲ ci si̲on²   Rule 13.

  en ti̲ tle̲₄

  po̲ li ti cal

⌈ na̲¹ tio̲n al

⌊ na̲ tio̲n

  re̲ cent

⌈ bu̲s̲² i ness   (Sound as written for spelling. We say "bi̲s² ness.")

⌊ bu̲s̲² y

  re fe̲r

min ute

mi nute

ought

ab sence

ab sent

con fer ence   (Does not follow Rule 15. The accent shifts to
con' and we do not double the r.)

con fer

Wed nes day   (Sound as written for spelling. This is Woden's
day. We say "Wens day.")

re al ly

re al

cel e bra tion

folks   (Sound l when spelling.)

folk

(This is the point of minimum accomplishment for a fifth grade.)

Section U

meant

mean

ear li est   Rule 24.

ear ly   (Page 2 in the Notebook.)

wheth er

dis tin guish   (Sound as written for spelling except you say
                          "gw" for gu. We say "dis ting gwish.")

con sid er a tion

col o nies   Rule 24. (Change y to i and add es.)

col o ny

co lo ni al   Rule 24.

as sure   (s says "sh.")

sure

re lief   (Page 3 in the Notebook.)

oc cu py

prob a bly

prob a ble

for eign   (Page 3 in the Notebook. ei says "ī.")

ex pense   Rule 20.

re spon si ble₄

re sponse₅

be gin ning   (Page 5 in the Notebook.)

be gin

ap pli ca tion

ap ply

dif fi cul ty

dif fi cult

scene   (These words use sc to say "s." Since e or i follows the c it must say "s." This can be likened

sci ence₃   to ck. c and k alone say "k" and when used together they say "k.")

scis sors

de scend

de scent

fi nal ly

fi nal

de vel op

cir cum stance₃   (Page 2 in the Notebook.)

cir cum fer ence₃

cir cle₄

is sue₂   (s says "sh.")

tis sue₂

ma te ri al

sug gest

mere

sen ate₅

sen a tor

sen a to ri al

re ceive₂   (Page 3 in the Notebook.)

re spect ful ly

re spect ful

re spect

a gree ment

a gree

un for tu nate₅

má jór i ty

ma jor

e lab o rate₅

cit i zen

cit y

né ces sa ry

né ces si ty

di vide

Section V   17

prin ci pal

prin ci ple₄

tes ti mo ny

dis cus sion   (Page 4 in the Notebook.)

dis cuss

ár range ment

ár range   (Here two separate consonants come between a
                    which says "ā" and the final e.)

ref er ence₃   (Rule 15 does not work here. The accent shifted
                        to the first syllable and we do not double the r.)
re fer

ev i dence

ex pe ri ence

ses sion   (Page 4 in the Notebook.)

sec re ta ry

as so ci a tion   (c and i are separate sounds. The syllable says "sĭ.")

ca reer

height   (We write an ā sound but we say "ī.")

weight

Section W

or gan i za tion

or gan ize

e mer gen cy

ap pre ci ate   (Page 4 in the Notebook. Since ci is a syllable alone it says "shĭ" instead of just "sh" as in ancient.)

sin cere ly

sin cere

ath let ic

ath lete

ex treme

prac ti cal

pro ceed

cor di al ly   (Sound as written for spelling. The British say
it this way.)

cor di al

char ac ter

      act

sep a rate

Feb ru a ry

li bra ry

Section X Y Z   /9

im me di ate

con vén ient   (The i says the consonant y sound as in opinion
shown before.)

re ceipt   (Page 3 in the Notebook. Sound the p for spelling. We do not say it in speech.)

pre lim i na ry

dis ap point

⌈ es pe¹ cial ly   (Page 4 in the Notebook.)
⌊ spe¹ cial

an nu al

⌈ com mit tee   (Except in a few words (recipē is an exception) we
                                use ee, ea or ey to say "ē" at the end of a word
│ em ploy ee   longer than she. Single e's are silent at the end of
                                other words.)
⌊ cof fee

⌈ de ci sion²   Rule 13.
⌊ de cide

prin ci ple₄

⌈ judg ment   (dg here does not follow Rule 3. This is an ex-
│   ception. The second spelling in the dictionary re-
⌊ judge   tains the e in dge but it is not commonly used.)

rec om mend

⌈ al lege₃
⌊ al le giance₃

The sixth-grade work should continue with and complete all of the Buckingham Extension to the *Ayres Spelling Scale.**

This Buckingham Extension adds words which are to be found in sixth-grade books and are needed in writing at that level. The Iowa Spelling Scale by E. J. Ashbaugh published by the University of Iowa at Iowa City is excellent for children who need help in analyzing words beyond those in the Ayres list. There is a separate booklet for each grade from the second to eighth.

The Ayres list is primarily one of base words and may be expanded by adding prefixes and endings. It is interesting to note that we recently had two second-grade classes, each of more than fifty pupils, who completed the Ayres list through the fourth-grade words. More than half made sixth-grade Metropolitan test spelling scores and not one of the 108 scored below beginning fourth grade. Thus children taught by this method do require supplemental word lists beyond the Ayres list for grades beyond the second.

---

*Public School Publishing Co., Bloomington, Ill.

CHAPTER VII

Teaching in the Different Grades

EVERY TEACHER from the first grade up should master the basic lessons of how to sit, how to hold a pencil, how to hold and move the paper, how to say the phonograms *accurately* and how to write the phonograms *correctly*. Then she should be responsible for seeing that *no* child is permitted to write without constantly being checked and taught these basic techniques.

The next step is to see that *all* children from first grade up can, and do, say the sounds first and write accurately at least their minimum part of the 1000 basic words in the Ayres list. The first grade teaches all the words in both the first- and second-grade lists. The second grade begins again with the first-grade list and at least goes through the third-grade list. The third grade begins again with the first-grade list and goes through the fourth-grade list. The teacher of each grade—even the eighth- or ninth-grade English teacher—should test her students beginning with the first-grade list and then go forward until she finds where each individual student, and the whole class, needs teaching. If she does not find a way to make up their deficiency in understanding how to say, write and read these basic words the child or group of children go into the next grade (or they repeat with no profit) still in a state of frustration as to language.

Teaching the words up to at least one year beyond his grade is necessary so that each child has a language tool sharp and complete enough to enjoy and do his work in mathematics, English, history and other studies. At every grade level then each teacher should hold herself accountable for teaching the basic elements of English to *all* in the class.

Every child tests constantly to see whether or not what he has learned works. If the teaching is based on facts he reasons as he learns. There should be no vague instructions, no telling him to guess at what the word must be, no looking at an illustration to see what it might be, nor merely seeing how it begins or ends, how long it is, etc., etc., ad infinitum! He must be taught how his language works and how the letters are used through logical reasoned teaching.

With this kind of teaching the child becomes quiet, self-assured, respectful of his teacher and the other children. He constantly competes with himself, trying to better his accomplishment. He accepts any suggestion for improvement gladly for as he *reasons,* he seeks any new light.

In classes of up to sixty children where this method of teaching is used, we have found all the children eager to be shown ways of improving their work. This attitude is not found in classes where teachers leave many children in the state that is conveniently labeled *"not ready,"* and where the range of accomplishment is so great that half and more of the children know they are not up to their grade standards. These children are not pleased with themselves, the teacher is not pleased with them, and their parents cannot be proud of their academic accomplishment. A child's mental health is much more assured when he knows he is or has a chance to get abreast of his classmates.

If a child is pleased with his academic accomplishments and still shows personality problems, then the school can look elsewhere for the cause of his problems. However, if he is not doing well in speech, writing and reading the school's first job is to teach the basic techniques to him. A systematic, scientific approach to his learning in school can show him how to attack other problems that beset him. This does not mean the school should not help a child in whatever way it can, but such help should not be a *substitute* for teaching him.

"Handedness" (i.e., being left-handed or right-handed) or "eye-edness" is not important if a child is correctly taught. What the child thinks he has said, seen or heard is important. Left-handed children need have no more difficulty in learning than do others.

Preschool Training

Nursery-school and kindergarten teachers, and parents at home before children go to school can answer a child's questions on how one says, writes or reads words by studying the previous chapters. Children want to write their own names at age three, four or five. They should be taught how to do so correctly, with a capital for the first letter and lower-case letters for the rest. They should be taught how to sit, hold the paper and the pencil, and how to sound out their own names. Whatever is given them should be intelligible and scrupulously correct.

In kindergarten children can learn to say the individual sounds of the phonogram cards, correlated with the correct writing of the symbols. This gives a basis for correcting their speech as from "stan" to *stand,* "jist" to just, etc. Children at this age are eager to learn, and if they are correctly taught the basis for a successful school life can be well laid. They come to school so that the teacher will *teach* them— not just to play or to express only that which they already know.

The First Grade

Learning to say the sounds of the seventy phonograms and learning to write correctly and legibly are two prerequisites to learning to spell and to read.

The teaching of writing, as described in Chapter IV, is combined with the teaching of the sounds of the phonograms right from the start. The teacher will use the blackboard as well as the phonogram cards, and explain the applicable rules.

Some children will write acceptably much sooner than others. As soon as half of the class has acquired enough skill—usually within an aggregate of ten to twelve hours of teaching time—the spelling of simple words should be introduced. Use the Ayres spelling list. The children write about ten new words a day in composition books strictly from the teacher's verbal dictation. Each day after the initial lesson, start with a written test given by dictating the previous day's ten new words in a changed sequence. The test is on a separate paper and the child does not see his errors again. When a child misspells a word on his test paper, the teacher checks this word in the child's notebook where the word is correctly written. He sees only his correct notebook. The checked words are his study lesson.

At every stage, and continuously, the teacher will require each child to *rewrite* each word in which his letters are not well formed or well placed, always asking him to state the rule or rules of writing which he has disregarded. The mental habit to remember and to apply the simple rules about sounding and forming the letters is important. He must learn to think. This is where the teacher must find time to help those who need extra teaching.

The above has to do with the formal spelling lessons. At other times during the day children's interest in how their names are written, words in connection with their play, trips, arithmetic, etc., should be taught. The children do the sounding and write on the board or on paper, with the teacher leading their recall of how the phonograms are made: Mar thå, Phil ip, rab bit, etc. Of course, the children learn that words cannot be written in syllables nor with phonograms underlined, etc. except in writing single words.

When (in about two months from the start of school) the class can read and explain a story of three or four sentences (written on the board without explanations), it is time to give them primers from which to read. It is an error to go too slowly and hold able children back.

The best primer I know is the HERE AND NOW PRIMER by Lucy Sprague Mitchell.* It tells of aspects of New York City which children find fascinating. It contains no illustrations. The children can draw their own pictures illustrating what they read. All other primers I know of are full of pictures. The children, when reading these, should be led to *read* the story first and *then* look at the pictures to see how well they illustrate the text.

Pictures are of great assistance when talking of something the children have not seen, but certainly no picture is needed for mother, father, cat, dog, house, automobile, etc.

When the first book is presented to a class, it should be read as an adult reads his book. Discuss the author. The children have been writing what *they* say. They have by now read three or four sentences about one subject written on the board by the teacher. They have discussed the meaning of the sentences. Similarly, the author of the book wanted to *talk* to children, so he *wrote* in the book what he wanted to say. He has a name for his book. What does he call it?

Discuss how we talk, not by saying one word at a time, but by saying together the words which go together for the sense of the sentence. How far does the author's first idea go? Where is the first period on the page? That shows where the author's first idea ends. What does the author say in that sentence? Show that the word before a period at the end of a sentence never can be read with the word beginning the next sentence. The sense of what is written is partially dependent on understanding the marks of punctuation.

Discuss the child's peripheral vision. Have each child hold his hands far out to the sides, look straight ahead and bring his hands in until he can see the tips of his fingers wiggle. He can see more than a yard across without turning his head. Therefore he can see the whole page at one glance since the page is not more than half a foot across. He can be led to *see* a sentence as a whole and thus read it as a complete thought—not word by word.

---

* E. P. Dutton, New York, 1936.

If the children have been properly taught to this point each child in turn should be able to read the ideas presented in the sentences with easy expression. Words that do present a difficulty should be sounded out as they are met. However, in reading *no* sounding out should be done aloud unless the child's silent sounding does not produce the correct word. Many teacher's manuals tell the teacher to present any new words to the class before they are met in the story to be read. They say that the one important thing is to get the meaning of the story. Children should get meaning, of course, but their habits of mind should be considered, too. They should work out the new words as they occur. No one is going to solve all their problems before each assignment when they are a little older. This telling them the new words fosters the mental habit which is seen in many children's inability to stick to an assignment, to concentrate in study periods, or on homework. Children need to be taught ways of meeting problems as they arise and *not* to look for an escape.

If the method given in this book is taught the child obtains in the spelling lesson the basic knowledge of how the written language works and he can figure out almost any word as he comes to it. If he needs some help the teacher helps him only on the individual sound he does not recognize. He should expect to work out each word with the minimum of help.

The teacher's homework is, in part, to see that there are no words in the reading lesson for which she has no explanation as to how they work phonetically.

In a half-hour unrehearsed television program which we gave over an N.B.C. affiliate a *second* grade that had had the Unified Phonics Method from the beginning of grade one read from a *fourth*-grade reader which they had not seen until they read aloud from it on the T.V. program. One boy in reading *buckles,* said, "buck, buck, buckles." He was the only one of the fifteen children who found it necessary to sound out a word. He and the others read smoothly and with true expression. They then answered well many questions put to them about what the story told.

I am quoting below from the report of a successful first-grade teacher on how she proceeds in teaching this method to her class of fifty-odd six-year-old children:

On the first day of school I showed the children how they should sit while writing, how to hold the pencil and how to use the "percolator," using the terminology of Mrs. Spalding. That term implies letting what they see or hear percolate (like water through the coffee) into their minds *before* they write or speak. The idea pleases them, and they get the point of thinking first, before acting. At the very beginning the habit of thinking, so necessary to success in learning, is being formed.

After that the single letter cards are the order of the day for about the first month of school. We review each day and add new ones, the number depending on the ability of the class. Provision is made for two half-hour periods each day. During these periods the children say the sounds and write on lined paper. One row at a time also writes on the blackboard. In this way the formation of the letters and the ability of each child to learn are checked.

After a few weeks most of the class is able to follow along as a group, and those who need extra help are singled out. When most of the children have a good idea of the single letter sounds and their correct written forms (that is, they can write them from dictation and not from seeing the cards), I proceed with the words in the Ayres list. The children continue with the other phonograms, for they must know all the sounds *before* the words containing them are presented. The first fifty cards are necessary to write all the first grade words in the Ayres list.

Last year I planned on thirty words a week and found it worked very well. The children sounded and wrote the thirty new words in their notebooks on Monday. We sounded out and then reread the first ten. These the children reviewed for homework. On Tuesday the children were given a twenty word test, ten review words and the ten they had studied. On Tuesday the children studied and sounded the second column of ten. The test on Wednesday included columns 1 and 2. On Friday they were tested on the thirty words. In this way those who were absent for a day or two were able to cover the material they had missed. It also helped the children who needed review. I found when I began to review the first and second grade words at the beginning of February that the children had really grasped them.

This year the children did not start the Pre-primer until November which meant they were then well into the second grade on the *Ayres Spelling List*. At the beginning I divided the class into two groups, 36 in my first group and 18 in my second. This enabled me to give those who needed less teaching a good start and to get them to work independently in their reading workbook. After Christmas when the first group had finished the Primer, I had them review for a week or so until the second group finished. The class started the First Reader together. I took half of the class at a time which meant only a half hour of teaching daily for each child. The children finished the First Reader before April. Now, in June, they have read the next three books. In reading supplementary material one group in the room never reads aloud a story already read aloud by another group. In this way each child has an opportunity to show he can read independently. All can do this. Some have read many library books during the year and have, because of it, much more expression and fluency. However, *all* can read and *all* comprehend.

At the beginning of February we started to review. Each day the children wrote five first grade words, ten second grade words (all review) and five third grade words (new) in five cent notebooks. These words were sounded by the children individually as they wrote them, then were read without being sounded out, and finally used in a sentence. Tests were given each day. The words spelled incorrectly were checked in their notebook and the per cent of errors written on the top of the page. In this way both children and parents could note progress and review, now and again, those words not mastered. (This would not have been possible if some eighth grade girls had not come to my assistance and corrected the spelling papers each day during their lunch period.)

The children begin after Christmas to compose and write their own sentences. In this way they learn to use a capital where they should and also to use a period or question mark at the end of each sentence. They like to illustrate their sentences in original art, which requires more thought about the meaning of words."

This teacher held a series of after school classes for parents. She taught them this method and they became a very real help, especially for the children who needed it most.

Second Grade

If the class has not been taught the Unified Phonics Method in the first grade, it is necessary to give them the entire first-grade work before going further, but this can be done more rapidly than with a first-grade group of children.

For classes who need only review this can be done in the first few weeks. The teacher will dictate words from the Ayres list and the children will, in concert, write them in composition books. The dictation and writing should be exactly as described by the directions given in Chapter V.

This and constant testing and review should be carried on until the class has learned to write correctly all words in the Ayres list for Grade II to Section M. A complete review should then be given, and for those ready for it the Grade III Ayres list should be started. This goes through Section O. In classes where this method was taught in the first grade many (more than half) have enjoyed working out the words through the fourth grade in the Ayres list. They find few words which are not already in their understanding and speaking vocabulary.

It is important that the teacher remember, at every stage and always, to point out every neglect of any of the rules of pronunciation, of writing, or of spelling which each child's work evidences, and to require him to state the rule and to make the correction himself.

Interesting, well written story books should be read aloud in class by second graders, not just "readers."

A teacher reporting in March about her second-year class says that she dictates 20 words each day (the children write them in their notebooks). Five words are from the first grade list, five from the second grade list, five from the third grade list and five from the fourth grade list. The first fifteen are review words. The last five are new. The next day they are tested on these.

This class learned cursive writing after Christmas. They learned to sound and write the seventy phonograms in cursive writing first, and then they wrote the Ayres list from the beginning. Once the cursive writing was introduced they did no more manuscript writing. When the Ayres list was dictated this time she taught them how to add endings to base words. She dictated the base word and then that word with any common ending: do, doing; last, lasted, lasting; old, older, oldest, etc.

In dictating words the teacher gives the word but the children give the sentence containing it. The teacher checks their understanding of the words and corrects any slovenly speech or incorrect sentence structure.

In February this group began reading from the McCall-Crabbs STANDARD TEST LESSONS IN READING—Book A. They read one lesson a day.

By April every child in this second grade could write at least two or three original sentences on a subject.

Third Grade

The third grade starts with a complete review of the first- and second-grade work. The children write for the first time the seven pages of the Child's Notebook in composition books for reference. Each child also enters in his notebook the words which he misses in the review of the first- and second-grade words from the Ayres list. This is his individual list. All the words of the third- and fourth-grade lists should be dictated by the teacher, and all children write all these words in the notebook. It is essential that the teacher continually repeat the spelling rules, correct the posture and writing habits, and at all times correct the pronunciation and the sounds and spelling of the phonograms.

Those children in the class who may not have had this method in the previous grade will need to start at the beginning and proceed more slowly than the others unless they learn rapidly during the review period at the start of the term.

It is advisable to seat such children and any others who have difficulty near the front where the teacher can supervise and guide them more easily. It has been found entirely practical to let the other children go ahead with reading to themselves and with other such work while the teacher works with the smaller group of children who need to learn spelling commensurate with their grade. All third-graders should learn the words at least to Column R. For most of the class there will be time to go through the rest of the 1000 words in the Ayres list.

The following is quoted from the report of a third-grade teacher:

For ten years I taught reading by the sight method using the program advocated in the teacher's guide book and followed scrupulously all the so-called "word skills" and "phonetic analysis drills." During this period I used two different readers which, although printed by separate companies, had practically identical systems for presenting vocabulary and word meaning. Likewise during this time I followed two different programs of spelling which stressed oral drill as well as peculiarities in the total word appearance. Five of those years were spent on the mainland and five here in Honolulu. However the entire period although a time of some success for two-thirds of the pupils, was (in the light of my later experiences using the Spalding Method) a time of frustration for one third of my pupils.

Reading, Writing, Spelling, English, and Phonics were each distinct subjects with no unifying bond. But I now find it quite easy to recognize the close connection between the written and spoken sounds in the English language. It seems so ridiculous for a child to read unhesitatingly the word "dog" for "puppy," or "dish" for "plate," and not even realize that he has made a mistake. Oral spelling certainly had its drawbacks too, for at the end of the year only one-fifth of the class were really masters of the four hundred words taught.

Mrs. Spalding's method gives all pupils an independence in attacking new words both in reading and spelling. My present class of sixty-one includes eight brand-new students who were not taught the Spalding method in grades one and two. On the second day of school I gave the Morrison-McCall Graded Spelling test. My median was 4.1, and all my eight new children, plus three of those exposed to the method for two years, were the only ones below 3.1. On October 7, I gave another Morrison-McCall test attaining the median of 5.2, with two of the new pupils still below grade level and also one of my repeaters. From September 1st to November 15th we have covered the entire Ayres list for grades one to three inclusive, and half of grade four.

As for reading comprehension the median on October 3rd was 4.5 and on Nov. 22nd, it reached 5.0. There isn't one non-reader in the class although there are a dozen children whom I give extra help on word meaning. Never do I tell any of the children a word that they can sound by using their phonograms. Exceptions are taught wherever they are met. I still help them on the "ough" card as it is confusing because of the six sounds. As for English Composition, I am simply amazed at what even the slowest can do. Some who learned spelling easily are writing plays. The majority take library books regularly and turn in book reports giving the title, author, characters, and a short appreciation of the book. Many are fast learning the art of using the dictionary to advantage.

Fourth and Higher Grades

Each class reviews and writes again the first seven pages of the Child's Notebook and is tested on the Ayres list from the beginning. Any words from the Ayres list which a child misses in the initial review he puts in his notebook and the teacher finds time to teach these to him as soon as possible. All children put all the words for their own grade and the grade above in their notebook. This shows the teacher where each child and the whole class needs teaching. When this is done, we shall not be sending children with second-grade spelling ability on to higher grades. If they have learned the structure of the language, reading can be taught with ease.

In classes where this method is taught in the first grade each child soon learns to write his own ideas in sentence form. In the second grade by March or April he writes short paragraphs daily. In the third grade he continues this and writes his own book reviews. At no time do the children copy from the board or out of books. Letters to parents and others, reports, etc. are individually composed and written from the start without copying. With this practice it can be hoped that high-school and college students will not dread compositions, nor essay questions in examinations, and that they will be at ease in speaking on subjects of which they have some knowledge. When children ask for the spelling of words they do not know, the teacher asks the child to sound the word and she corrects any inaccurate sounds. The child writes the parts of the word he can and the teacher helps only with those parts he does not know. From third grade on the dictionary should be used when the teacher is not readily available.

Speed reading, which is currently being widely taught, is suitable only, in my opinion, for children who have really learned to read; that is, to read accurately. It is no substitute for the basic teaching of the language subjects.

It should be stated that foreigners studying English will quickly acquire a grasp of our language if it is presented along the lines of this method in the phonetic manner. Without this logical approach English is one of the most difficult languages even for those whose native tongue is a Latin or Germanic language. I have taught a few teachers who are now using it with great success in Japan, the Philippines and in Polynesia.

The teachers using the Unified Phonics Method have found the Morrison-McCall Spelling Scale for Grades 2 to 8 very useful. This scale is published by the World Book Company at Yonkers-on-Hudson, New York, and 2126 Prairie Avenue, Chicago. There are eight parallel tests of 50 words each. Each teacher, beginning in February of the first grade, and in September for the second and subsequent grades, should use one of these tests on the first of each month. This regularly shows how each child is progressing and does not put off until the end of the year learning that some children need special attention.

For reading test lessons we have found McCall-Crabbs STANDARD TEST LESSONS IN READING a great help. There are five booklets for grades 2 through 12. Each booklet contains some 70 paragraphs with about ten questions on each paragraph to be answered. Each test is a three-minute one and the grade scores are given for each test. They are published by Teachers College, Columbia University in New York City.

Unless a teacher has some way of knowing at frequent intervals, other than by subjective judgment, how her children are progressing much time is lost in helping those who need it most.

Many parents have become interested in mastering the techniques of this method and have organized for regular class sessions. These parents are of invaluable assistance to teachers.

When I have taught individual children who have difficulty in the language subjects, I have required that the parents of children of elementary-school age especially work with the child and me through the lessons so that they can help their children at home. This can make for a strong bond between children and parents. When a parent does not know how to help, he is placed in the unhappy role of a task-master. Teachers should feel responsible to parents for giving them any information they have which parents can use at home to help their children learn.

So many parents have told me that primary teachers say to them, "Don't teach your child at home. You will only confuse him. Let the school teach him to read." Then when the school has not taught him to read, teachers say, "Help him at home," or "Get a tutor for him." They often give the parents no idea as to *how* to help and no word as to just what the tutor should do. There is much untapped assistance for the teacher in the parents of the children who need more help if these parents are taught how.

How should each child study the words he misses?

1) Read the word carefully, sounding each sound of a one-syllable word and each syllable of a polysyllabic word.
2) Cover the word and write it, sounding the individual phonograms or syllables.
3) Check to see that the word is correct. This self-testing habit is very important.
4) Do this with each word to be learned.
5) Ask a "reliable" person at home or in school to test him on the new words exactly as tests are given in class.
6) The tester should check the paper as the teacher does.

7) The child immediately restudies by writing the words missed.

8) Repeat these tests until the child no longer makes errors in writing these words. *whole test (different order)*

9) Bring to class the next day the study sheets, the home test, and further study sheets if any.

Here is something definite which teachers can teach parents. They can invite parents to the children's classrooms and have them participate in the lessons. They learn how to hold the paper and the pencil, how to sit, how to form the letters, saying the sound before the writing of each phonogram. The teachers explain how spelling is taught and just how the parents can help their children in reading, in spelling or in speech. In the end this cooperation relieves the teacher of much special attention to pupils who need the most help.

High-school students who have not been taught by this method can benefit greatly from it as the following quotation from a teacher's recent report indicates:

After two months' work last fall with my five senior English classes, I realized that the students were not able to go ahead with a regular 12th grade curriculum without special assistance from somewhere. They misspelled simple words. Most of them approached English and reading—as though it were impossible of comprehension by any normal being.

The teaching of Old and Middle English literature to people who could not read present-day English was highly improbable and I found the students blithely flunking exams with grades of 10 and 20 rather than attempting to do the homework connected with literature.

Some of them could quote grammar rules, name parts of speech and even diagram sentences with easy fluency but they could not write. I found I could not teach composition because they did not have the tools for self-expression.

Vocabulary was just as hopeless. They reacted with resentment when they found that there were shades of meaning for the correct usage of a word.

The first spelling tests I gave showed the same incomprehension. After the first two letters, a word, to most of them, was simply a wild jumble of letters which carried no meaning either to their eyes or their ears.

The result was that I stopped all regular work in English and started the students out on a six-weeks' course of Mrs. Spalding's method. We made notebooks, using the first seven pages as a graphic presentation of the rules of spelling. Then we started on lists of spelling words which commenced with grade 1.

Although they started the new regime somewhat rebelliously, the students soon recognized that the sounding of the letters was not only teaching them spelling, but correct speech sounds without the embarrassment of working in front of a group. As they began to comprehend the letters by sound, the English language began to fall into order in their minds and they began to find that they had a whole new grasp of their own language. This was apparent to me in the growing unity and cooperation in the classes. For the first time I was not pulling against them.

Soon students began coming to my desk and expressing appreciation of the work I was giving them, telling me that they had never been taught like that before. One boy told me, "If I could spell, I could learn to read!"

The results of the first spelling test showed that the average grade level of these senior high school students was between sixth- and seventh-grade. If I had given the first test before we started on Mrs. Spalding's regime, the average would have been probably at fifth grade. On the second test, given a month later, the average rose about half a grade level. But the mistakes consisted of only one letter in a three-, four-, or five-syllable word. The average of the class in spelling has risen steadily until time for their college entrance examinations.

About one-third of the whole senior class has taken the college entrance examinations (the highest number yet to do so in the history of the school).

The good students have become much more secure; the poor students are by now passing in their 12th grade work. None of this would have been possible if I had not been able to give the students a grounding in the English language. During the first two months I was failing with them, as other teachers before me had failed. And I would still be failing if I had not had this concise, logical and most readily teachable method to present to my classes. Giving my students this work has solved not only their most obvious problems in speech and the use of English but also the more subtle problems of courtesy and class behavior. I simply do not have the disciplinary problems that bedevil so many of my colleagues.

CHAPTER VIII

Specific Disabilities

THERE IS ONE more phase of teaching the English language which requires special mention.

Teachers in all grades encounter many children with definite reading or spelling handicaps. Dr. Orton evolved his method—which is essentially the basis on which I have developed my method of teaching *all* children—to overcome these handicaps in children having severe disabilities. Some insight into his discoveries and teaching will be helpful to both parents and teachers of such children.

Following World War I Dr. Orton discovered that soldiers who had lost the ability to speak, read or write because of head wounds could regain these abilities by certain training. In brief, he learned that on both sides of the human brain there is a center where the picture of words seen on the printed page is recorded and where meaning is given to them. On one side the image is in reverse from that recorded on the other side. Therefore one side should become the dominant one, the one habitually used. Which side is the dominant one is a matter of inheritance much as (although entirely independent of) inherited left-handedness or right-handedness. If the other, or less dominant, side is sometimes used the child records the letter or letters in reverse. At such times the young child mistakes b for d, was for saw, on for no, etc. Al-

228

though the older child may learn to correct this for short words he becomes utterly confused by longer ones. His reading (and spelling) is thus, in many instances, pure guesswork. These children have simply inherited a tendency to use not one side, but either side of the brain for identifying meaning with the printed words seen. The same sort of confusion occurs with children who cannot decide whether to jump from the right foot or the left. They are not well coordinated in certain physical efforts. Motor patterns are stored in other areas of the brain, but in the same way that the symbols of written language are recorded. This is why it is necessary to teach handwriting—the motor patterns— so thoroughly.

This tendency to use sometimes one, sometimes the other side of the brain, and sometimes both at once in reading can only be overcome by training these children to use habitually one side only. This is done by reinforcing their uncertain visual recall with the use of their aural recall and their kinesthetic controls. The latter are usually not uncertain when the visual recall is. For that reason the child is taught to use the muscles of his mouth to say the word, and those of his hand to write it, and he hears it at practically the same time that he sees his own writing of it. That is why children should say a syllable just before they write it. Suffice it to say that, regardless of theory, this process actually works and works infallibly for all children.

Some, of course, need more of this training than others. Note that the teacher quoted in the previous chapter gave eighteen children in her group more of this basic training, while the thirty-six others went ahead more rapidly until the eighteen caught up. It takes much longer for these children to acquire a dominant side of the brain if they start this training in later years.

Fully one-fourth of any group tends to have, under today's teaching methods, this sort of reading disability and barely ten per cent are likely to be entirely free from it. It has nothing to do with a child's intelligence. I have tested literally hundreds of slow readers and found this tendency to be confused and similar signs of this particular trouble in nearly every one. Thus it is not remedial teaching for a few, but a suitable method for all, and the elimination of all remedial reading cases, which we should aim for, especially since this method of teaching is no handicap to any, and is fundamentally sound for every child.

I have just tested a bright boy entering third grade who had not been taught by this method. His tests showed the typical errors of a child with this specific confusion in language. In reading he scored 1.4 instead of 3.0. Some of his errors were that he read dig, big; dug, bus; cart, card; of, from; who, will; how, low; tan, tell; tap, teeth; done, doing; left, light; form, from; balk, black; pig, big; sung, sun; and send, san.

In spelling he scored 1.9. He wrote soft, sf; spent, sbt; deep, be; stay, stat; upon, ap; street, steen; and his name Clarke, Clke and then Clkic. He made most of the horizontal lines backwards. These errors are clear evidence of the source of his trouble. His visual recall of what he reads is often in reverse; and his inability to express in letters the sounds of words in his spelling is apparent.

It is interesting to note that Dr. Orton and most other students of this problem have concluded that this confusion in the visual recall of words read is inherited through the maternal side, as is color-blindness. This is said to account for the fact that about four times as many boys as girls have serious trouble in reading. I believe it is a fallacy that this reading difference is caused by a slower maturing of boys' minds. As I have said, the weight of evidence indicates that every school child is physically and mentally mature enough to read at about the age of six.

We have not said much about the fact that good speech, at least as regards accurate, clear pronunciation, is essential to the best results from this method of teaching, and is its most valuable by-product. Otto Jespersen said, as quoted earlier, that in English the consonants are clearly and concisely pronounced. Yet today in America, as another scholar points out, how many teachers have fallen into the current lazy habit of pronouncing consonants in a slovenly and indecisive manner. Many people reduce to a minimum the movements of the organs of speech, and their language becomes a confused noise of words, so indistinguishable as to be very difficult to understand.

I can compare the ease with which a large audience understood the speaking (without loudspeakers) of the English concert comedienne, Anna Russell, and the great difficulty in understanding a very eminent American doctor, speaking with the latest amplifying devices in an acoustically perfect auditorium to a much smaller audience.

If our consonants are being slighted in American speech how much more are we neglecting the accurate sounds of the vowels. The one sound "uh" is frequently substituted for many of the true vowel sounds. Our American spoken language has been rapidly deteriorating, and this has probably come about chiefly through the fact that this generation has been given no clear understanding of the phonetic basis of English. The relation between the spelling and the pronouncing of every word has not been taught or even explained. That relationship, however, is the key to this method of teaching, and accurate speaking is a definite, important part of this teaching. It should be said further that the habit of using clear, easily understood speech is a real aid to clear thinking. Also, while it may not exactly win friends, it certainly helps in influencing other people. The standards of accurate pronunciation which a teacher requires of her pupils are really a very important part of their education. It may not be too late to stem the present trend in America toward the serious deterioration of our spoken language.

On this point teachers and educators need to know that the dictionary upholds no standard of pronunciation. Instead its only aim is to reflect the average pronunciation of educated people, including some parts of their present slovenly and deteriorating speech in the United States. We ought therefore to speak more precisely than the dictionary indicates—that is, to follow more precisely the correct vowel sounds and avoid the slurring of consonant sounds.

Children who have inherited the tendency to severe language disabilities will overcome this in the first grade if properly taught, but if this method is not available for them until much later on they will still overcome it with good classroom teaching and a little home cooperation. They should not need any remedial teaching by a special teacher.

CHAPTER IX

Final Uses and Objectives

IT HAS BEEN my objective to write a book which is constructive, to give parents, teachers and educators, and our children something directly useful. I have tried to avoid the more exhilarating process of deflating the various false gods of language teaching to whom so many educators make obeisance. Other books have ably exposed the serious failure of current reading methods, and it has been my purpose to present a solution to the problem. It is my hope that this resulting book is sufficiently complete and clear to enable both teachers and parents to follow and teach from it accurately without any added instruction.

In the very interesting scheme of things, whereby mankind individually spends but a few days, relatively speaking, on this fairly permanent globe, it naturally befalls us to pass on to children what we have learned in life. Otherwise mankind recedes instead of advancing towards its ever expanding destiny.

But teaching is not only the most important duty of each generation; it is also the most delicate of all arts. A gifted teacher always needs to be extremely sensitive to her pupils' emotional and mental processes. What holds their attention, what best reaches their understanding, what helps them retain, what inspires them to make use of and apply regularly all that they learn?

It has been of absorbing interest to learn some of the answers to these questions by careful trial and error in the field of teaching language. I have approached the problems on the perhaps unfair assumption that all big and little prevailing ideas on how to teach every part of language ought to prove out under test, and that minor, if not major, improvements might be attained by careful testing in practice.

That is why this book may seem to parents and to some trained teachers to be unnecessarily full of detailed teaching techniques. All of them are, however, good working techniques and worth recording.

As I have said repeatedly, our immediate aim is the teaching of accurate speaking, good handwriting, correct spelling and easy, rapid and fully understood reading, but it cannot be said that this is our final objective. These are only the tools to which every child is entitled and which are absolutely essential to the mental and spiritual development of his maximum inherent abilities. Many other things are needed to bring forth the best in a man, but without these basic tools at his command he cannot begin to realize his natural capabilities. Many fine minds are denied their full growth and contributions to mankind simply because they lack mastery of these basic means of communication from others (as in reading), and with others (as in speaking and writing).

Let me illustrate how an early mastery of the language arts by a class provided enough free time so that I was able to teach history and related subjects in the manner which I think is ideal. My sixth-grade group of 32 in the Bronxville Public School near New York City read aloud together six excellent story books on the Middle Ages.

I purchased seventeen copies of each and had two children sit together as we read them. Each of these books was very well written.

We thus built a *common* background on the Middle Ages. We said such words as *tournament, battlements, moat, illuminated manuscript, scriptorium, falcon;* and for each concept I had scoured the old bookshops of New York for the best illustrations available. Old illustrated musical periodicals yielded some beautiful pictures of monastic life in color. Art books had reproductions in color of Brother Stephen's illuminations for the very Hour Book told of in GABRIEL AND THE HOUR BOOK by Evaleen Stein (L. C. Page, Boston). Each picture was of artistic merit.

I took a course for teachers at the Metropolitan Museum of Art on background material that the Museum offered, to make such studies as the medieval period come alive for children. The staff at the Museum also provided invaluable bibliography and source material. At Columbia University I took many courses in Industrial Arts from Miss Sara Patrick and Miss Florence House, now with the Arts Cooperative Service. They taught me how the monks made ink and paints, how to bind a medieval book, how to weave a small Oriental rug, how to weave a small Gobelin tapestry, how to work in metal and with leather, how to make the natural dyes as they were made in the Middle Ages, how to make stained glass, etc. These crafts were to be used for true education work. The intellectual content was unbelievably rich.

These studies together with my straight history courses made my sixth-grade students able to enjoy our work on the Middle Ages. They formed guilds, made banners, wrote their laws, became apprentices, journeymen and master craftsmen in weaving, dyeing, metalwork, leatherwork, etc. They saw how these guilds were the forerunners of today's labor unions. Each child made a cartoon, using appropriate subject matter. Then with the same number of warp threads to the inch and the same kind and weight of wool as those in the Metropolitan Museum, each student wove a tapestry about five by eight inches. When we visited the Museum they all had some idea of the work involved in making those beautiful tapestries. Each child wrote, illuminated and bound a book. When we went to the Pierpont Morgan Library and saw probably the finest collection of illuminated books in the world, they looked at them with genuine appreciation.

The children embroidered, using long, narrow cloth and wool of the same colors as were used in the Bayeux tapestry. Our tapestry told the story of GABRIEL AND THE HOUR BOOK instead of the Norman Conquest.

At the end of the year the children wrote and produced a play using properties we had been making. The pupils' language was colored by the fine writings we had read together.

Some children read as many as fifty books on the Middle Ages. I had seen to it that they had the kind of knowledge which made exciting and interesting reading of such books as THE STORY OF KING ARTHUR AND HIS KNIGHTS by Howard Pyle (Scribners, New York).

I have written briefly on what my sixth-grade class in history did to show how one of the real interests in teaching is to give children a share in our great cultural heritage. This group learned dozens of our finest poems—poems they will be proud to know when they are many years older. They wrote copiously on their experiences and on the books they read independently. They learned and their interests expanded and they took on new depths of understanding, not only of history but of the present-day world. They learned something about the start of this scientific era and developed this further in their science classes.

What has all this to do with phonics? The answer is simply this: Without a working knowledge of how to speak, write and read any child is severely handicapped in learning of and understanding his cultural heritage.

Such studies can be started as early as the third grade. For example, third-graders can carry out a rich study of the American Indians with real intellectual content. After reading aloud together books that give in story form the lives of the various tribes and studying geography which partly explains why one tribe lived quite differently from another, children can then read individually as many as a hundred books on Indians. One of my third-graders did just that by February of one year. He was quite an authority for an eight-year-old. An excellent series for reading aloud together are the books on Indian life by Sonia Bleeker (William Morrow & Co., New York). THE INDIAN'S SECRET

WORLD by Robert Hofsinde (William Morrow & Co., 1955) is an excellent source book.

All children can enjoy enriched education if speech, writing, spelling and reading are taught in the first two years by the method recommended in this book. Those who cannot speak well, read intelligently and write well hold back the imparting of knowledge and true education to the whole class. When we water down education to the level of those who present learning difficulties, we neglect the education of those who learn with ease. Thus the true objective for a teacher is to avail herself of the means of raising the standards of all children in a group so that all may enjoy a good education.

This sort of enriched teaching in the elementary school prepares children to study intelligently straight history, economics, foreign languages and similar courses in high school.

These supplementary parts of teaching are obviously open to parents, just as the techniques in this book of teaching the language arts can be taught at home. Even when children may be taught in the classroom it is a great help to have parents understand and cooperate at home.

An educator has recently written, "It is hoped that some day education will throw away meaningless generalizations and concentrate critically upon the learning that takes place." That has been my endeavor. I also agree with him that teaching should provide each child with the tools and interests which enable him to learn and grow intellectually. A democracy especially requires a type of universal education which will develop in each individual his maximum ability for understanding and sound thinking.

I am, as I write this closing word, about to begin teaching my method to a group of sixty public- and private-school teachers and a few mothers. It will require forty hours in class to prepare each of them to teach it to children successfully. I estimate that a serious student of this book will need the same time to achieve a similar ability to teach it.

It is thus our hope that the book may, in effect, enable anyone or any groups of teachers and parents to learn and use this method. It follows then that our major objective in this undertaking may be accomplished.

This objective is to help prevent the unhappiness and the appalling loss caused by so large a proportion of our people living and thinking, working and producing, at levels so far below their inborn mental abilities, because of their relative inability to read and write. As a corollary to this objective we also hope for an important up-grading in the average standards of scholarship and educational objectives in all our schools and colleges. We believe we have presented in this book one indispensable, basic step toward attaining these two great goals.